Practical Guide to the Operational Use of the AK47/AKM and AK74

By Erik Lawrence

Copyright ©2014 Erik Lawrence

Erik Lawrence

www.vig-sec.com   erik@vig-sec.com

Printed and bound in the United States of America

First printing 2006
Second printing 2014

ISBN-10: 1-941998-01-1
ISBN-13: 978-1-941998-01-4
E-BOOK-ISBN-13: 978-1-941998-57-1
LCCN: Not yet assigned

I0170701

ATTENTION US MILITARY UNITS, US GOVERNMENT AGENCIES AND PROFESSIONAL ORGANIZATIONS: Quantity discounts are available on bulk purchases of this book. Special books or book excerpts can also be created to fit specific needs. For information, please contact:

Erik Lawrence

www.vig-sec.com   erik@vig-sec.com

CREDITS:
Wikipedia contributors, "Main Page," Wikipedia, The Free Encyclopedia, http://en.wikipedia.org/w/index.php?title=Main_Page&oldid=83971314 (accessed October 7, 2006).

Firearms are potentially dangerous and must be handled responsibly by individuals. The technical information presented in this manual on the use of the AK series rifles reflects the author's research, beliefs, and experiences. The information in this book is presented for academic study only. Neither the author nor the publisher assumes any responsibility for the use or misuse of information contained in this book.

SAFETY NOTICE
Before starting an inspection, ensure the weapon is cleared. Do not manipulate the trigger until the weapon has been cleared of all ammunition. Inspect the chamber to ensure that it is empty and no ammunition is present. Keep the weapon oriented in a safe direction when loading and handling.

AMMUNITION NOTICE - these weapons fire the 7.62 x 39mm (AKM/AK-47) not the 7.62 x 54mm Russian or the 7.62 x 51 NATO (.308 Winchester), and 5.45 x 39mm (AK-74), not the 5.56 x 45mm NATO (.223 Remington). Firing the incorrect ammunition will damage the weapon and possibly injure the operator.

Training should be received from knowledgeable and experienced operators on this particular weapons system. Vigilant Security Services, LLC provides this training and continually perfects its instruction with up-to-date information from actual use.

PREFACE

This manual is intended to be a reference for those involved in the use, maintenance and instruction of the featured firearm. My aim in writing these manuals is to set the record straight and dispel many of the false assumptions related to the different firearms. The early sections of the manual contain background material on the featured firearm which allows the user to gain the basic building blocks for further education. The firearms featured in these manuals have been used for decades by our allies and enemies, and will be for the foreseeable future, so why are we not experts with them? If I am fighting with the firearm or providing instruction on a firearm, I want to use and know their system better than they do.

The rationale for writing these manuals comes from the fact that there are not libraries of easily accessible references to use in developing your own training system for these firearms. Many of the old military field manuals are decades old and were incorrectly translated by someone who had no idea what the firearm could do, let alone basic firearm knowledge. We started from the ground up and developed the manuals to provide instruction in progressive steps that could be easily grasped and continually referred back to. A good grounding in the basics of firearms, safety, and instruction allows the user to use these manuals to their maximum value. A competent user will find little difficulty in interpreting and applying the information in the manual to their own training program.

The guide goes through the most fundamental parts of the firearm in detail and more advanced techniques are not covered as extensively. With this in mind the user can use these principles and adapt it as needed to their required level of instruction. The emphasis of this guide is in acquiring familiarity with the fundamentals of all firearms and learned competence rather than becoming a firearms guru.

Many of the points in these guides were developed from scratch in theatres of conflict and are continually improved and updated for each edition. I have continually used vetted points from users and professionals in the guides to continually update them to the best known practices for each particular firearm. If it is valid and relevant we will include it in the next edition.

Please note that this guide assumes some familiarity with the basic concepts in firearm safety, gun handling skills, common sense and an ability to process new information. Readers should have knowledge of the difference in calibers, countries of origin, and the knowledge of the priority of the skills needed for development.

I hope you find this work useful and remember that a manual does not replace proper training and hands on experience. Please email comments to w , particularly if you find any errors or glaring omissions.

Erik Lawrence

Table of Contents

AK-47

ASSAULT RIFLES

AK-74

Section 1

AK/AKM 47/74 Operator Manual Introduction

The objective of this manual is to allow the reader to be able to competently use the AK/AKM 47/74 weapon systems. The manual will give the reader background/specifications of the weapon; instructions on its operation, disassembly and assembly; proper firing procedure; and malfunction/misfire procedures. Operator level maintenance will also be detailed to allow the reader to understand and become competent in the use and maintenance of the AKM rifles.

AK/AKM 47 Description

Weapon Specifications -
- Mode: Select Fire (Semi and Full Automatic)
- Operation: Gas operated, rotating bolt with 2 lugs
- Cartridge: 7.62 x 39mm
- Weight (empty magazine without ammunition):
  o AK-47 - 4.3 kg/9.5 lbs.
  o AKM - 3.14 kg/ 6.9 lbs.
- Overall length: 87 cm/34 inches
- Cyclic rate of fire: 600 rpm
- Combat effective range: 400m

Feed
- Ammunition magazine capacity: 30- and 40-round magazines in both metal, plastic, and Bakelite construction
- 75-round drums for the RPK from multiple countries
- Magazine lock up is a hook-front-and-rock-back-to-lock type

Barrel
- Length: 41.5 cm/16.3 inches
- Muzzle velocity: 710 m/s/2330 fps

Sights
- Front - protected cylindrical post
- Rear - rectangular notch, tangent ramp
- Rear sight graduation - 100-800 (AK) or 1000 (AKM) meters in 100-meter increments; battle setting is approximately 250 meters.
- Adjustment - front sight for zero only and rear sight for elevation

Action

- Locking feature is a rotary bolt
- Select fire from the closed bolt
- Safety type is a lever selector with safe, semi-automatic, and automatic-fire settings.
- Safety location is on the right side of the receiver above the trigger guard.

AK/AKM 74 Description

Weapon Specifications
- Mode: Select Fire (Semi and Full-Automatic)
- Operation: Gas operated, rotating bolt with 2 lugs
- Cartridge: 5.45 x 39mm
- Weight (empty magazine without ammunition):
  - AK-74M - 3.4 kg/7.5 lbs
- Overall length: 940 mm/37 inches
- Cyclic rate of fire: 600-650 rpm
- Combat effective range: 500 m

Feed
- Ammunition magazine capacity: 30- and 40-round magazines in both plastic and Bakelite construction
- Magazine lock up is a hook-front-and-rock-back-to-lock type.

Barrel
- Length: 415 mm/16.3 inches
- Muzzle velocity: 910 m/s/2950 fps

Sights
- Front - protected cylindrical post
- Rear - rectangular notch, tangent ramp
- Rear sight graduation - 1000 meters in 100 meter increments; battle setting is approximately 250 meters.
- Adjustment - front sight for zero only and rear sight for elevation

Action
- Locking feature is a rotary bolt
- Select fire from the closed bolt
- Safety type is a lever selector with safe, semi-automatic, and automatic-fire settings.
- Safety location is on the right side of the receiver above the trigger guard.

AK/AKM Background

Figure 1-1

The AK family of rifles are gas-operated, rotating-bolt, closed-bolt firing, and select-fire rifles.

AK-47 (*Автомат Калашникова образца 1947 года, Avtomat Kalashnikova 1947*) is a gas-operated assault rifle designed by Mikhail Kalashnikov, produced by Russian manufacturer Izhevsk Mechanical Works and used in many Eastern bloc nations during the Cold War. It was adopted and standardized in 1947. Compared with the auto-loading rifles used in World War II, the AK-47 was generally more compact, with a shorter range, a smaller 7.62 × 39mm cartridge, and capable of selective fire. It was one of the first true assault rifles and remains the most widely used. The AK-47 and its numerous variants and descendants have been produced in greater numbers than any other assault rifle and are in production to this day.

The AK-47 design work was completed shortly after World War II, as can be seen by the origin of its model number (47 representing the year in which its design was adopted and given its current designation); and it was in service in the Soviet army from the early 1950s, the beginning of the Cold War period. The design was influenced by contemporary and previous weapons like the FG-42, the MP-44 (later renamed Stgw-44), and early Russian attempts to build a lighter automatic rifle based around the Japanese 6.5mm Arisaka round, such as the AVS-36 Simonov and the early 1916 Avtomat by Fedorov. The AK-47 was adopted as the standard issue infantry weapon of the Soviet army due to its firepower, ease of use, low production costs, and reliability, which fit the Soviet doctrine of Operational Art; as well as being suited for the new mobile warfare doctrines. The AK-47 was widely supplied or sold to nations allied with the USSR, and the blueprints were shared with several friendly nations (the People's Republic of China standing out among these).

The AK-47 was designed to use the production methods that were state-of-the-art in the Soviet Union in the late '40s. This detail implied that it more or less used the same methods of construction as used for the PPSh-41 and the PPS-43. A common misconception is the claim that the AK-47 was derived from the German Sturmgewehr-44, which it was actually not (however, the Sturmhewehr-44 had some good ideas which contributed somewhat to the design). The design of an automatic rifle was in the works in Russia, before World War II even began. The Avtomat Kalashnikov barrel, bolt, and receiver was also milled out of a block of steel (that was changed to metal stampings), adding to its durability but also the weight of the rifle. In order to be able to use a steel grade that was easy to machine, the barrel and bore were hard chromed. The stock was simply made out of wood, which was a non-strategic material. This perfectly fit into the Soviet manufacturing philosophy, where large plants using much untrained labor could manufacture basic weapons cheaply and in very large quantities.

Another feature that is typical of Soviet-designed assault rifles is the capability of the AK-47 to keep working no matter how dirty it gets. This feature can be attributed to the bad experience the Soviet Union had during the early stages of WWII, where it lacked proper ammunition-production facilities. Thus, until 1943, the Soviet Union was reduced to using some very poor powders in its ammunition that left much residue in the guns. The Soviets also had learned early on that during a major conflict, there is little time to train soldiers to keep their weapons clean.

Over time, the AK-47 descendants have been simplified through the use of spot welding and by further reducing the number of machined parts. The Izhevsk factory that manufactures the AK-47 descendants like the AK-100 can manufacture around 8,000 units per night shift or around 24,000 units per day). Because of its design, it is not possible to manufacture the AK-47 series efficiently in small micro plants due to the large amount of metal stamping equipment needed for mass production. However, the AK-47 has been copied and manufactured in small shops all around the world, at the expense of many more man hours per unit.

Variants of AK Style Rifles

Several variants of the AK exist; the AK has become a true combat rifle. The following are of some of the variants:

Figure 1-2 AK-47

- **AK-47, 7.62 × 39mm** — (*Автомат Калашникова образца 1947 года*, pronounced *Avtomat Kalashnikova 1947*) is a gas-operated assault rifle.

Figure 1-3 AK-47 1948-51

- **AK-47 1948–51, 7.62 × 39mm** — The very earliest models with the Type 1 stamped sheet metal receiver are now very rare.

Figure 1-4 AK-47 1952

- **AK-47 1952, 7.62 ×39mm** — Has a milled receiver and wooden buttstock and handguard. Barrel and chamber are chrome plated to resist corrosion. Rifle weight is 4.2 kg.

Figure 1-5 Chinese Type 56

- **Chinese Type 56, 7.62 ×39mm** — Chinese copy of the AK-47 Kalashnikov. The rifle exists in three variants; Type 56 (with fixed stock), Type 56-1 (with under-folding stock) and Type 56-2 (sideways-folding stock). This series of rifles is most easily identified by the folding "spike" bayonet attached to the barrel just aft of the muzzle.

Figure 1-6 AKS-47

- **AKS-47, 7.62 ×39mm** — Featured a downward-folding metal stock similar to that of the German MP40 for use in the restricted space in the BMP infantry combat vehicle.

Figure 1-7 RPK

- **RPK, 7.62 × 39mm** — Squad automatic rifle version with longer barrel and bipod. **RPK** (*Ручной пулемёт Калашникова,* pronounced *Ruchnoy Pulemyot Kalashnikova*) is the light machine gun that replaced the RPD in the role as squad automatic weapon for Soviet infantry. This weapon can fire all the AK/AKM magazines to include the 30-, 40-round magazines and the 75- round drum. The receiver is identical to that of the AK-47 except for bulges on the sides of the forend to accommodate matching bulges in the front trunnion which add strength to the design. The weapon's stock is different to allow for more comfortable and effective use during prone firing. The barrel is also longer and heavier to provide more reliable and accurate performance during heavy usage and automatic fire. The weapon's rear sights are also different, allowing for windage adjustment. A paratrooper variant called the RPK-S had a side-folding stock.

Figure 1-8 AKM

- **AKM, 7.62 × 39mm** — A simplified, lighter version of the AK-47; Type 4 receiver is made from stamped and riveted sheet metal. A slanted muzzle device was added to counter climb in automatic fire.

Figure 1-9 AKMS

- **AKMS, 7.62 × 39mm** — Folding-stock version of the AKM intended for airborne troops. Stock may be either side- or under-folding

Figure 1-10 AKM w/ GP-25

- **AKM with GP-25** — 40mm under-barrel grenade launcher. The grenade launchers fire a series of special 40 mm grenades. Originally, the main grenade was the VOG-15 (7P17) fragmentation grenade. This was superseded by the steel-cased VOG-25 fragmentation grenade. A bounding grenade, the VOG-25P is also available; on impact, a small charge in the nose of the grenade is detonated, which raises the grenade 0.5 to 1.5 m in the air before an impact delay fuse detonates it. Smoke grenades are also available, initially a grenade called GRD-40. Now a series of smoke grenades designed for use at different ranges called GRD-50, GRD-100 and GRD-200 (for use at 50, 100 and 200 meters, respectively). They are capable of producing a 20-meter cube of smoke that lasts for one minute in winds up to five meters per second. A CS gas grenade called the Gvozd and a baton grenade are also available.

Grenade Launcher Specifications
- Caliber: 40 mm
- Weight: 1.3 kg (GP-30), 1.5 kg (GP-25)
- Length 276 mm (GP-30), 323 mm (GP-25)
- Performance:
    - Muzzle velocity: 76 m/s (250 ft/s)
    - Rate of fire: 4-5 round/min.
    - Sighting range: 400 m (1300 ft)

Grenades
- Fuze arming range: 10-40 m (33-130 ft)
- Fuze self-destruction time: 14-19 seconds
- VOG-25 specifications:
    - Weight: 250 g/0.55 lb
    - Warhead: 48 g of A-IX-1 explosive
- VOG-25P specifications:
    - Weight: 278 g/0.61 lb
    - Warhead: 37 g of TNT
- GRD-50/100/200 specifications
    - Weight: 265 g/0.58 lb
    - Warhead: 90 g charge

Figure 1-11 AK-74

- **AK-74 series,** 5.45 × 39mm — In 1978, the Soviet Union began replacing its AK-47 and AKM rifles with a newer design, the AK-74. This new rifle and cartridge had only started being exported to eastern European nations when the Soviet Union collapsed, drastically slowing production of this and all other small arms. Buttstock has a groove cut into both side for low-light recognition.

Figure 1-12 AKS-74

- **AKS-74,** 5.45 × 39mm — side-folding skeleton stock for airborne and specialized troops.

Figure 1-13 AK-74M

- **AK-74M,** 5.45 × 39mm — The latest variant, issued to the Russian troops since the early 1990s. Key differences from the earlier AK-74 rifles are the side-folding plastic buttstock and the scope-mounting rail on the left side of the receiver. Buttstock has a groove cut into both side for low-light recognition.

Figure 1-14 AKS-74U "Krinkov"

- **AKS-74U,** 5.45 × 39mm — *Krinkov* (also referred as ***AKSU-74*** or ***AK-74SU***) was introduced in the 1970s. The AKS-74U short assault rifle (the "U" suffix means *Укороченный,* pronounced *Ukorochennyj*" in Russian and meaning shortened in English) was developed in the late 1970s from the AKS-74 assault rifle. It is basically the shortened version of the AK-74 assault rifle and combines the small size of a submachine gun and relatively powerful ammunition (which is the same as used in the classic AK-74 rifle). A notable distinguishing feature is its conical flash suppressor. The AKS-74U has the size and effective range of a typical submachine gun but has the advantages of general issue and assault-rifle ammunition and magazines, as well as the parts interchangeability with the general issue assault rifle, the AK-74.

It was intended for use by vehicle crews, artillery teams, and Special Forces, which needed a small and lightweight weapon. A special version of the AKS-74U had been developed for Spetsnaz, which could be fitted with a quickly detachable suppressor and a special 30mm suppressed grenade launcher model BS-1 pronounced *Tishina* meaning (silence). The launcher uses special HE-DP grenades, which are launched using special blank cartridges stored in the box magazine contained in the launcher pistol grip. The rear sight is a flip-type U-notch, while the front sight is a cylindrical post and can be fitted with night sights.

The AKS-74U has only a few differences from the basic AKS-74 assault rifle. The AKS-74U has a severely shortened barrel, with the gas chamber moved back and an appropriately cut down gas piston rod. Since the portion of the barrel after the gas port is very short, a special muzzle device was designed, which is used as a flash hider and the gas expansion chamber (to achieve reliable gas-operated action). The front sight base is lowered, and the standard adjustable rear sight is replaced by the flip-up rear (marked for 200 and 400 meters distance), mounted on the receiver cover. The receiver cover is hinged to the receiver at the front and flips up when opened (original AK-74 receiver cover is detachable). Otherwise the

AKS-74U is similar to the AKS-74; it has similar controls, folding buttstock, and uses same magazines. AKS-74U cannot be fitted with a bayonet. Some versions had a standard side-mounted rail for the night or red-dot scopes and are known as AKS-74U-N.

Figure 1-15 RPK-74

- **RPK-74,** 5.45 × 39mm — The RPK-74 had been developed along with the AK-74 assault rifle as a squad level light-support weapon for the new, small-caliber ammunition, 5.45 x 39mm. The RPK-74 had been adopted by Soviet Army in late 1970s and is still in use by the Russian army, usually issued as one item per infantry squad (10 men).

The RPK-74 internally is almost the same AK-74 rifle-select-fire, gas-operated, rotating-bolt locked firearm with heavier and longer non-removable barrel, bipod, and redesigned buttstock. RPK-74 can be fed from 45-round box magazines or standard AK-74 30-round box magazines; 75-round drums, similar in design to those of RPK, were also developed.

Versions of the RPK-74 with side-mount for IR (night vision) scopes are called RPK-74N. Earlier RPK-74 were manufactured with a wooden hand guard and fixed buttstock. Most modern RPK-74s are manufactured with a polymer hand guard and side-folding polymer buttstock. Statistics: weight, 5kg/11 pounds with the bipod; length 1060mm/41.7 inches; length of barrel 590mm/23.2 inches; rate of fire is 600 rounds per minute.

Figure 1-16 AK-101

- **AK-101 Series,** 5.56 × 45mm — The AK-101 is an assault rifle of the Kalashnikova series. The AK-101 is designed for the world-export market, using standard 5.56 x 45mm NATO cartridges, which is the standard of all NATO armies. The AK-101 is aimed at those looking for the logistical compatibility and familiarity of the 5.56 x 45 NATO round with the proven quality and reliability of a Kalashnikov. Potential customers may be Western-oriented countries looking for just that. It is designed with modern and composite materials, including plastics that reduce weight and improve accuracy. Many of the improvements found in the AK-101 are also present in the AK-103 and the rest of the AK-10X series of rifles. Buttstock has a groove cut into both side for low-light recognition.

The AK-101 can be fired in semiautomatic and fully automatic modes. The disassembly procedure for the AK-101 is identical to that of the AK-74. The AK-101 has an optical plate installed on the side of the receiver for attaching scopes and other optical equipment, which will accept most types of Russian and European AK optics. The rifle accepts most synthetic and metal ammo magazines with a 30-round capacity. The AK-101 has a 16-inch barrel with an AK-74 style muzzle brake attached to the barrel to control muzzle climb.

A common misconception is that the AK-101 has entered service as the main assault rifle of the Russian Federation, but this is not true, the AK-74M is still the main assault rifle, with the AN-94 entering limited service in the elite forces of the Russian military, some Russian police forces, and the Internal Ministry of Affairs.

Figure 1-17 AK-102

- **AK-102,** 5.56 × 45mm — The AK-102 is chambered in 5.56 x 45mm NATO and features black synthetic furniture, with a side-folding stock. The side-folding stock looks just like a normal fixed stock, however it folds and locks securely to the side of the receiver. The AK-102 has a 12-inch barrel with a Krinkov style muzzle brake to allow the action to cycle. Due to the shorter barrel length of the rifle, the gasses escape faster and don't allow a new round to be chambered. The Krinkov muzzle brake is used to trap the gasses and allow the action to cycle. The AK-102 can be fired in three different firing modes; semi-automatic, three-shot burst and full-automatic. The AK-102 has an optical plate installed on the side of the receiver for attaching scopes and other optical equipment. The optical plate will accept most types of Russian and European AK optics. The AK-102 has a rate of fire of 600rpm.

Figure 1-18 AK-103

- **AK-103,** 7.62 × 39mm — The AK-103 is a modern Russian-built version of the famous AK-47 assault rifle, chambered for the 7.62 x 39 mm round. It combines the developments made in the later AK-74 and AK-101 with a use of plastics to replace metal or wooden components wherever possible to reduce overall weight.

The AK-103 can be fitted with a tactical light, laser sight, scope, and suppressor. The AK-103 is in limited service with selected units in the Russian army and is already being exported to other countries, such as Venezuela.

Figure 1-19 AK103K

- **AK-103K,** 7.62 × 39mm — 14.3-inch barrel plus compensator and AK-74 style compensator. Features a 30-round magazine, plastic folding butt, mount on the receiver for night sights, plastic fore grip, handguard and pistol grip.

Figure 1-20 AK-104

- **AK-104,** 7.62 × 39mm — 12.3-inch barrel plus compensator and AKS-74U style compensator. Features a 30-round magazine, plastic folding butt, mount on the receiver for night sights, plastic fore grip, handguard and pistol grip.

Figure 1-21 AK-105

- **AK-105,** 5.45 × 39mm — 12.3-inch barrel plus compensator and AKS-74U style compensator. Features a 30-round magazine, plastic folding butt, mount on the receiver for night sights, plastic fore grip, handguard and pistol grip.

Figure 1-22 AK-107

- **AK-107/108 Series,** 5.45 × 39mm/5.56 x 45mm — The AK-107 and AK-108 are variants of the AK-101 series. The difference from the lower numbered series is that the 107 and 108 have BARS (Balanced Automatic Recoil System) based on the AL-7. As the projectile is ejected from the muzzle, the gas that flows into the main gas chamber moves toward the piston that drives the bolt. This actions occurs while another portion of the same gas moves through its own cylinder to a piston that moves in the opposite direction, towards the muzzle. This "double recoil" decreases recoil and increases accuracy in full auto mode. The 107 and the 108 are different in that the 107 uses a 5.45 x 39mm cartridge while the 108 uses a 5.56 x 45mm NATO cartridge. Like the rest of the 101 series, these newer AKs use synthetic materials, such as black fiberglass-reinforced polyamide, for the pistol grip and heat shield. This change of material is more cost-efficient and much stronger than the original AK-47 wood furnishings.

Figure 1-23 Iraqi Tabuk

- **Iraqi Tabuk AK rifle,** 7.62 × 39mm — The Tabuk is a collective name for all Iraqi license-produced 7.62 x 39mm AK rifle variants; the Iraqis never made any in 5.45 x 39mm calibers. This series of rifles came about when Yugoslavia provided the process and equipment to the Iraqis in the 1980s. They are modeled off the Yugoslavian Zastava M70 series with a sniper version, full wooden stock infantry version, a heavy barrel model RPK type, and the underfolding model version. They can be distinguished from other AKs by their unique pistol grips made from plastic and their gas block/sight post. They are heavier weapons since they are on milled receivers but seem to be durable and reliable. It has been our experience that not all AK magazines lock into the receiver so prepare your load accordingly.

Figure 1-24 VSS AKs

VSS AK—the most modernized AK rifle available

Special Operations Forces (SOF) requires the capability to adapt basic issue weapons to meet several mission needs. The VSS AK Accessory Kit provides the AK47/74 Rifle with the flexibility and versatility to meet SOF mission-specific requirements. Items contained within the VSS AK Accessory Kit increase the weapons lethality through fire control and target acquisition both day and night during Close Quarter Battle (CQB) and up to ranges of 500 meters. Options are in all calibers normally manufactured in the AK series.

Kits can be custom fitted with the accessories of your choice on many of the common models of the AKM series rifles and short-barreled carbines.

Base Weapon modifications available for the VSS AK system
- Upswept charging handle (early models)
- Tritium "Night-Sight" for front sight post
- Tritium rear sight with windage adjustment

- Enhanced magazine catch release (early models)
- Enhanced selector lever with bolt-locking notch
- **Vortex® flash eliminator** (AK47 models only)
- Integrated 5-rail mounting system - Four rails on the front of the weapon at the 3, 6, 9, and 12 o'clock positions, and the fifth rail on top of the receiver
- Canted vertical grip -This grip was specifically designed to have a more natural feel and to be out of the way for magazine changes on the AK rifle.
- Harris or other type rail mounted bipod
- Collapsible stock or side-folding skeleton stock
- Ergonomic pistol grip

Optional:
- 40mm grenade launcher - The VSS AK47/74 can also make use of a rail mounted 40mm grenade launcher
- Pelican/Storm hard case for maximum portability and protection

General Characteristics

Figure 1-25

AK Rifle Construction

The AK-47 is simple, inexpensive to manufacture, and easy to clean and maintain. Its ruggedness and reliability are legendary. The large gas piston, generous clearances between moving parts, and tapered cartridge case design allow the gun to endure large amounts of foreign matter and fouling without failing to cycle. This reliability comes at the cost of accuracy, as the looser tolerances do not allow the precision and consistency that are required of more accurate firearms. However, it is important to bear in mind that although accuracy was not the feature most desired of this design, it is still present. Reflecting Soviet infantry doctrine of its time, the rifle is meant to be part of massed infantry fire, not long-range engagements.

The bore and chamber, as well as the gas piston and the interior of the gas cylinder, are generally chromium plated. This plating dramatically increases the life of these parts by resisting corrosion and wear. This point is particularly important, as most military-production ammunition during the 20th century contained corrosive mercuric salts in the primers, which mandated frequent and thorough cleaning in order to prevent damage. Chrome plating of critical parts is now common on many modern military weapons.

Technical description for the AKM assault rifle:

The AKM is a gas-operated, selective-fire assault rifle. The gas-operated action has a massive bolt carrier with a permanently attached long-stroke gas piston. The gas chamber is located above the barrel. The bolt carrier rides on the two rails, machined or stamped in the receiver, with the significant clearances between the moving and stationary parts, allowing the gun to operate even when its interior is severely fouled with sand or mud. The rotating bolt has two massive lugs that lock into the receiver. The bolt is so designed that on the unlocking rotation, it also makes a primary extraction movement to the fired case, resulting in very positive and reliable extraction even with a dirty chamber and cases. The rotation of the bolt is ensured by the curved cam track, machined in the bolt carrier, and by the appropriate stud on the bolt itself. The return spring and a spring guide are located behind the gas piston and are partially hidden in its hollow rear part when the bolt is in battery. The return spring base also serves as a receiver cover lock. The cocking handle is permanently attached to the bolt carrier (in fact, it forms a single machined-steel unit with carrier) and does reciprocate when gun is fired.

The receiver of the AKM is made from the stamped sheet steel, with machined steel inserts riveted into the place where required. The earliest AK-47 receivers were also made from stamped and machined parts, riveted together, but this method soon proved to be unsatisfactory, and most of the AK (pre-1959) rifles were made with completely machined receivers. The receiver cover is a stamped sheet metal part, with stamped strengthening ribs found on the AKM covers.

The relatively simple trigger/hammer mechanism is loosely based on the 1900s-period Browning deigns (much like most other modern assault rifles) and features a hammer with two sears-one main, mounted on the trigger extension, and one for the semi-automatic fire that intercepts the hammer in the cocking position after the shot is fired and until the trigger is released. An additional auto sear is used to release the hammer in full-auto mode. The AKM trigger unit also featured a hammer release delay device, which is used to delay the hammer release in the full auto fire by few microseconds. This does not affect the cyclic rate of fire, but allows the bolt group to settle in the forward most position after returning into the battery. The combined safety - fire selector switch of distinctive shape is located on the right side of the receiver. In the "Safe" position (topmost), it locks the bolt group and the trigger and also serves as a dust cover. The middle position is for automatic fire, and the bottom position is for single shots. The safety/fire selector switch is considered by many as the main drawback of the whole AK design, come custom firearms is addressing this deficiency. It is slow, uncomfortable and sometimes stiff to operate (especially when wearing gloves or mittens), and, when actuated, produces a loud and distinctive click. There's no bolt stop device, and the bolt always goes forward when the last shot from the magazine is fired.

AKM is fed from the 30-round, stamped-steel magazines of heavy, but robust design. Early AK magazines were of slab-sided design, but the more common AKM magazines featured additional stamped ribs on the sides. A positive magazine catch is located just ahead of the trigger guard and solidly locks the magazine into the place. Insertion and removal of the magazine require slight rotation of the magazine around the front top corner that has a solid locking lug. If available and required, a 40-round box magazine of similar design or the 75-round drums (both from the RPK light machine gun) can be used. Late in production plastic magazines of the distinctive reddish color were introduced.

AKM rifles were issued with wooden stocks and pistol grips. Late production AKM rifles had a plastic pistol grip instead of wooden one. The wooden buttstock has a steel buttplate with mousetrap cover that covers the accessory container in the butt. The AK buttstock is more swept down than the AKM ones. The folding stock version had been developed for the airborne troops, and it had an under-folding steel shoulder stock. These modifications of the AK and AKM were designated the AKS and AKMS, respectively. AKs were issued with the detachable knife-bayonets, and the AKM introduced a new pattern of the shorter, multipurpose knife-bayonet, which can be used in conjunction with its sheath to form a wire-cutter. All AK and AKM rifles were issued with the leather or canvas carrying slings.

AK/AKM Sights

The notched rear-tangent iron sight is adjustable, each setting denoting hundreds of meters. The front sight is post adjustable for elevation in the field. Windage adjustment is done by the armory prior to issue. Sight tools are now available to let operators quickly zero the rifle to their shooting positions. The battle setting places the round within a few centimeters above or below the point of aim out to approximately 250 meters. This "point-blank range" setting allows the shooter to fire the gun at any close target without adjusting the sights. Longer settings are intended for area suppression. These settings mirror the Mosin-Nagant and SKS rifles, which the AK-47 replaced. This feature eased transition and simplified training. The AK-47 rear sight is graduated from 100m to 800m, and the AKM is graduated from 100m to 1000m, with 100m increments and 250m battle sight setting. The scope mounting rail is located on the left side of the receiver on some models. **The replacement peep sight below listed greatly enhances the accuracy of the typical AK rifle as the eye more naturally centers the front sight using a peep sight, especially in conjunction with the tritium replacement front sight.**

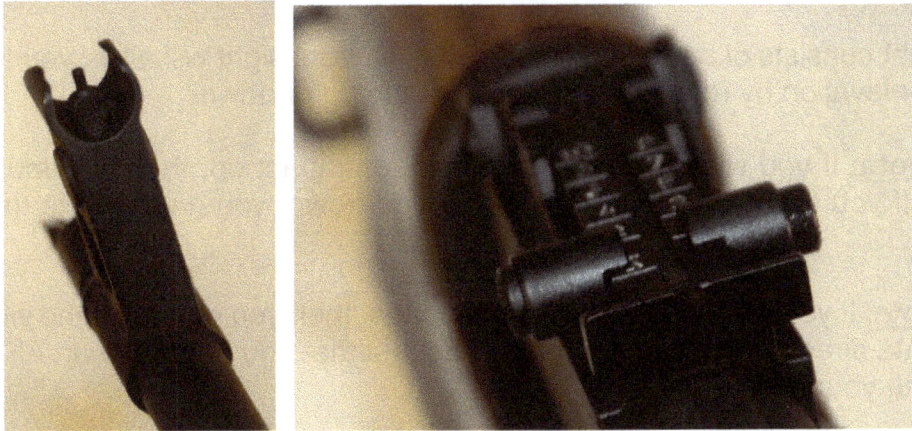

Figure 1-26a and 1-26b Photo of standard front and rear sights

Figure 1-27 Photo of standard sight alignment

Figure 1-28 Sight picture through a Krebs Custom AK Peep Sight

Zeroing the AKM-type rifle

Zero procedure: Attempt to do this on a known distance range on a windless day from a solid bench rest.

AK-47/AKM-type rifles have one adjustable sight, which is the front. Zeroing elevation adjustments and windage adjustments are made using the front sight. The rear sight is set up for a battle sight zero setting and 1-8 or 1-10 (hundreds of meters increment) with the slider. The tangent rear sight has a slider that has pre-calibrated elevation adjustments for different ranges. With tangent sights, the rear sight is often used to adjust the elevation once calibrated, and the front to adjust the windage.

Some models (RPK usually) have an adjustable rear sight on which you can zero your windage. The rear sight has an elevation slide with range indicators from 100 to 1000 meters. Elevation is controlled by moving the slide in the up or down position. You can also use this sight on your AKM if you replace it so as to keep your front sight post centered and adjust your windage on the rear sight.

The front sight consists of a rotating sight post. The front sight will allow you to adjust and calibrate for elevation by rotating the front sight pin up or down.

Elevation Note: If you wish to move your point of impact up, then you must rotate the sight down. If you wish your point of impact to go down, you must rotate the front sight pin up.

Windage Note: If you wish to change your windage, then you must drift the windage drum in the opposite direction desired. I strongly suggest that you purchase an AK sight tool; it makes drifting your front sight much easier.

Front Sight Note: Any changes you make on your front sight must be made in the opposite direction.

Establish Battle Zero

The following procedure will establish a zero at 14 meters (near) and 230 meters (far) for 7.62x39mm and 21 meters (near) and 250 meters (far) for the 5.45x39mm. This procedure will be for establishing a battle zero and will also calibrate your range indicators on the rear tangent sight with the slider. For these two zeros, you will keep your rifle on the lowest slider setting, which has different characters to denote battle zero. Different countries mark this setting differently, but "П" is a Cyrillic P for program (zero) in Russian. Remember, these are iron battle sights, and the rifle is made to be an under-300-meter-battle rifle – not a group shooter, but a man shooter.

Establish Mechanical Zero
- Slide the spring-loaded slider down the tangent sight until the range scale П mark is aligned with the top of the slider.

- Carefully aim and fire each shot of a 3-shot group at a paper target set up at 14 meters for the 7.62x39 and 21 meters for the 5.45x39 caliber. If your shots are not striking the point of aim, then adjust your sights.
- To raise the next shot group, rotate the front sight post in the down direction (clockwise).
- To lower the next shot group, rotate the front sight post in the up direction (counter-clockwise).
- To move the next shot group left, turn the rear sight windage knob counterclockwise, or drift the front sight to the right.
- To move the next shot group right, turn the rear sight windage knob clockwise, or drift the front sight to the left.
- Continue to fire 5-shot groups and adjust the sights until you have a tight group at the point of aim.
- Once you complete this step, the rifle is now combat-zeroed; all other ranges on the elevation scale are also zeroed, so to engage target at, say 500 meters, slide the spring-loaded slider to 5.
- Once the weapon is zeroed, you can set the slider on the battle sight zero for shooting from 0-300 meters without changing the elevation. While using a battle zero, you will have to remember your ballistics and adjust your hold if shooting the mid range. Example, if you are shooting at 175m, you will have to hold slightly lower as this is around the maximum ordnance (highest point in the bullet's arc). My rule is to hold for belt line at any mid range and squeeze the trigger.
- VSS developed an AK47/AKM zero target for making this process much simpler. They have a grid system to allow for accurate adjustments using the sight tool to speed up zeroing.

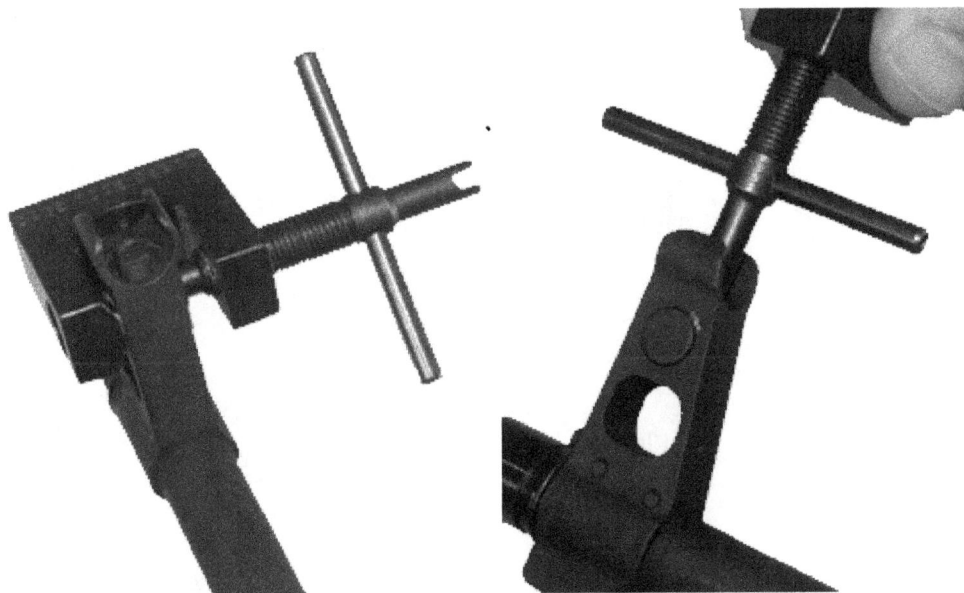

Figure 1-29a and 1-29b Photos of front sight windage and elevation being adjusted with the sight tool

100-meter zero (Remember, the farther away it is, the harder to dial in.)
If you are zeroing at 100 meters on setting one at 100 yards, one full rotation of the front sight (elevation) will shift point of impact 6.7 inches. One full rotation of the windage adjustment will shift point of impact 9.4 inches. These calculations are based on the standard length AK barrel.

Ballistic Reference Stock Charts

I print, laminate and put these charts on the stocks of my rifles for quick reference. Holds are in inches.

7.62x39mm	
Holds with a 14m Zero	
Dist. (m)	Hold (in.)
14	0
50	-3
100	-6
150	-6
200	-3
230	0
250	+3

5.45x39mm	
Holds with a 21m Zero	
Dist. (m)	Hold (in.)
21	0
50	-2
100	-4
150	-4.5
200	-3
250	0
300	+5

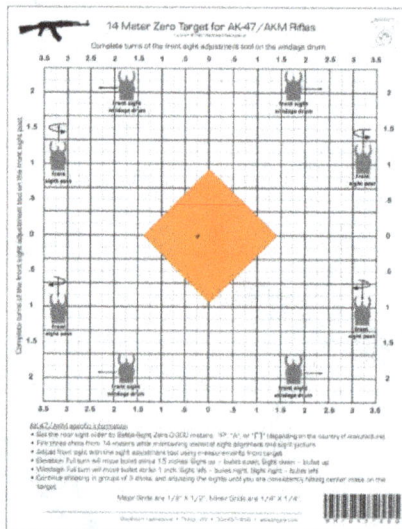

Figure 1-30 AK47 Zero Target

Aftermarket replacement sights and sight tool

AmeriGlo Tritium Front Sight
Item Number VSS-AK-715

AmeriGlo Tritium Rear Sight
Item Number VSS-AK-981R

Krebs AK Rear Peep Sight
Item Number VSS-KCI-006

VSS AK Sight Adjustment Tool
Item Number VSS-001-181

AK/AKM-47- 7.62 x 39mm Ammunition

The Soviet **7.62 × 39mm** rifle cartridge was designed during World War II and first used in the SKS carbine. The cartridge was influenced by the late-war German 7.92mm *Kurz* (*Kurz* meaning short in German). Shortly after the war, the world's most recognized assault rifle was designed for this cartridge: the AK-47. The cartridge remained the standard Soviet load until the 1970s and is still by far the most common intermediate rifle cartridge used around the world. Its replacement, the 5.45 × 39mm cartridge, is less powerful but longer ranged (due to its much higher velocity) and is more controllable in full-auto fire (due to the lower recoil). The change was a response to the NATO switch from the 7.62mm cartridge to 5.56 x 45mm NATO.

Ballistics
The standard AK-47 or AKM fires a 7.62 × 39mm round with a muzzle velocity of 710 m/s (2,329 ft/s). Muzzle energy is 1,990 joules/1,467 ft-lb. Cartridge case length is 38.6 mm; weight is 18.21 g. Projectile weight is normally 8g/123 grain. The AK-47 and AKM, with the 7.62 × 39mm cartridge, have a maximum effective range of around 300 meters. For comparison, the 7.62 × 54mm R cartridge has a projectile of 9.6-12 g/148-185 grain [depending on the weapon]) at a velocity of 818m/s (2,683 ft/s) for approximately 4,000 joules/2,950 ft-lb of energy.

The original Soviet bullets are boat-tail bullets with a copper-plated steel jacket, a large steel core, and some lead between the core and the jacket. The cartridge itself consists of a Berdan-primed, tapered steel case which seats the bullet and contains the powder charge. The taper makes it very easy to feed and extract the round, since there is little contact with the chamber walls until the round is fully seated. This taper is what causes the AK-47 to have distinctively curved magazines. While the bullet design itself has gone through a few redesigns, the cartridge itself remains largely unchanged.

This cartridge has endeared itself to shooters in spite of its limited ballistics, which are analogous to the .30-30, because of the many very inexpensive good semi-auto rifles (notably the SKS) available for it.

M43 Bullet Design
Although the new cartridge represented a great leap forward from previous designs, the initial bullet design was flawed. The complete solidity of the M43 projectile causes its only drawback—it is stable even in tissue and begins to yaw only after traversing nearly 30cm of tissue. This characteristic greatly reduces the wounding effectiveness of the projectile against humans. Dr. Martin Fackler noted that the wounds from the M43 round were comparable to that of a small handgun round using non-expanding bullets. Unless the round struck something vital, the wound was usually small and quickly healing. Extremity hits were seen as nearly inconsequential.

M67 Bullet Design
In the 1960s, the Yugoslavians experimented with new bullet designs to produce a round with a superior wounding profile to the M43. The Yugoslavian-type rounds are known as

M67 and incorporate an air gap inside the front of the bullet that shifts the center of gravity rearward, causing the bullet to destabilize nearly 17cm earlier in tissue. This feature causes a pair of large stretch cavities at a depth likely to cause effective wound trauma. When the temporary stretch cavity intersects with the skin at the exit area, a larger exit wound will result, which takes longer to heal. Additionally, when the stretch cavity intersects a stiff organ like the liver or a full bladder, it will cause damage to that organ.

However, without fragmentation, the wounding potential of M67 is mostly limited to the small permanent wound channel the bullet itself makes. While a fragmenting round (like the 5.56 x 45mm) might cause massive tissue trauma and blood loss (and thus rapid incapacitation) on a lung or abdominal hit, the M67 has a greater chance of merely wounding the target. Still, it is an enormous improvement over the M43 design.

Nearly all modern 7.62 x 39mm rounds of civilian or military manufacture are of the M67 variety—a simple boat tail FMJ round with a forward air cavity. Notable exceptions are the Ulyanovsk Machine Factory EM1 "match" (which substitutes a nipple for an air cavity and produces a single large temporary cavity in place of two small ones) and the Wolf 150 grain/9.7 gram soft point, which behaves much more like a traditional expanding hunting round. Nearly all Jacketed Hollow Point rounds in 7.62 x 39mm are M67 rounds with a small hole in the front of the jacket—terminal ballistics are nearly identical to their fully jacketed brethren. They are a concession to various hunting laws that forbid FMJ rounds. Of all the tested JHP rounds, only Ulyanovsk EM3 hollow points seem to expand at all.

Chinese Steel Core
Chinese military-issue ammunition in this caliber is M43 style with a mild steel core and a thin jacket of copper or brass. Contrary to common belief, the use of steel was a cost-saving measure rather than one to increase the penetration. Additionally, mild steel is not sufficiently hard to grant unusual armor-penetrating capability. Despite this, Chinese ammunition is currently banned from importation in the US because that there are 7.62x39mm caliber "handguns" (mostly Krinkov pistols and a few single-shot target pistols), and the ammunition is an "armor-piercing handgun round" under the U.S. federal legal definition of the word, which is based on materials and bullet design rather than on tested ability to penetrate armor.

Other Names for 7.62 x 39mm
On some occasions, this ammunition is referred to as 7.62mm Soviet, 7.62mm Warsaw Pact rounds, or 7.62mm ComBloc. It was also known in the United States as .30 Short Russian; the "Short" was to distinguish it from the older .30 Russian (7.62mm Russian), which was the 7.62 x 54mm R.

Since approximately 1990, the 7.62 x 39mm cartridge has seen some use in hunting arms in the US for hunting game up to the size of whitetail deer, as it is approximately as powerful as the American .30-30 Winchester round and has a similar ballistic profile. Large numbers of inexpensive imported semi-auto rifles, like the SKS and semi-auto AK-47 clones and variants, are available in this caliber, and the SKS is so inexpensive as to have begun displacing the .30-30 lever-action rifles as the new "poor person's deer rifle." Inexpensive imported 7.62 x 39mm ammunition is also widely available, though much of it is of the non-expanding type that may be illegal to use for hunting in some states. However, a number of American civilian manufacturers produce soft-tip rounds, suitable and legal for hunting.

The 7.62 x 39mm ammunition used by the AK/AKM is produced by Russia, former Soviet republics, China, and many different European countries. The 7.62 x 39mm cartridges will be encountered in both brass and steel cases; however, steel cases are more prolific. The 7.62 mm is the diameter of the bullet and 39mm is the length of the case.

The following is a brief list of the different types of ammunition and their uses:

- Steel-core ball - for use against light material targets, personnel, or during training. The steel-core ball weighs 122 grains. No tip markings.

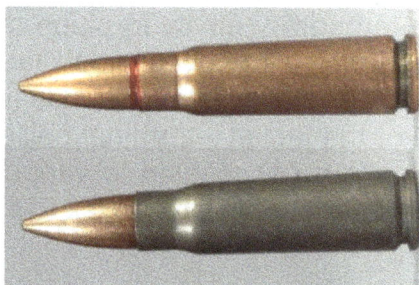

**Figure 1-30 Photo of standard 7.62 x 39 ammunition
steel case - top and lacquered case - bottom**

- Tracer - for observation of fire, incendiary effects, signaling and for use during training. Green-tipped marking and primer painted green denotes the green trace when fired. No photo available.

- Armor piercing - for use against lightly armored targets where armor piercing effects are desired. Black tipped marking. No photo available.

- Blank - for use during training when simulating live fire. If blanks are to be fired from the AKM Rifle, a blank adapter must first be fitted to the muzzle. Without the blank adapter, insufficient gas pressure is generated to cycle the weapon properly. Crimped nose. No photo available.

Ammunition Identification

7.62 x 39mm examples

Figure 1-31 Ball	**Figure 1-32** Ball	**Figure 1-33** Tracer	**Figure 1-34** Frangible	**Figure 1-35** Soft Point

Caliber, mm	Case	Bullet type	Bullet, wt. Grain	Primer Type	Description
7.62 x 39	Bimetal	Bimetal	122	Berdan	Steel Core
7.62 x 39	Bimetal	Bimetal	122	Berdan	Steel Core
7.62 x 39	Bimetal	Tracer T-45M	122	Berdan	Tracer Bullet
7.62 x 39	Brass	Frangible	125	Boxer	Frangible
7.62 x 39	Brass	Soft Point	125	Boxer	Soft Point

Standards for small arms ammunition are given below.

Color	Type
None	Ball L (lead core)/Ball PS (steel core)
Yellow	Heavy Ball D
Yellow/Silver	Heavy Ball D (steel core)
Silver	Light Ball LPS (Steel core) - Obsolete
Green	Tracer
Black	AP
Black/Red	API
Black/Yellow	API - Obsolete
Purple	AP-T
Purple/Red	API-T
Red bullet with black tip	API (Carbide core)
Red/Red primer	HEI
Black/Green	Reduced velocity (Sub sonic)
Crimped extended case	Blank

7.62 x 39mm 122 grain ball ammunition

BC: 0.3 G1   CAL: 0.308 in   WGT: 122 gr

MV: 2330 ft/s   CH: 10 ft

WS: 10 mph   TS: 10 mph

T: 59 °F   PC: 29.92 in Hg   H: 0%   A: 0 ft

SH: 1.5 in   SO: 0 in   ZH: 0 in   LOS: 0°

Range	Drop		Wind		Lead	
(m)	**(in)**	**(moa)**	**(in)**	**(moa)**	**(in)**	**(moa)**
100	7.0	6.2	1.7	1.5	26.4	23.1
200	5.5	2.4	7.5	3.3	56.9	24.8
250	**-0.0**	**-0.0**	**12.1**	**4.2**	**73.8**	**25.8**
300	-9.4	-2.7	18.1	5.3	92.1	26.8
400	-42.5	-9.3	34.4	7.5	133.1	29.1
500	-99.9	-17.4	56.9	9.9	180.3	31.5
600	-188.8	-27.5	85.3	12.4	233.4	34.0
700	-316.3	-39.5	118.6	14.8	291.4	36.3
800	-488.8	-53.4	156.0	17.0	353.5	38.6

7.62 x 39mm Ballistic chart

AK/AKM-74 - 5.45 x 39mm Ammunition

The Soviet 5.45 × 39mm M74 round was introduced into service in 1974 for the AKSU-74 carbine/sub-machine gun and the AK-74 assault rifle, which is an updated version of the AK-47. The round, which replaced the AK-47's 7.62 × 39mm round then in Soviet service, was likely developed based on Soviet observation of the American 5.56 × 45mm round in Vietnam.

The Russian military-issue 5N7-specification 5.45 mm bullets are a somewhat complex full-metal-jacket design. Some people have said that the Russians were concerned about the lower energies of the bullets and designed them to cause more damage than might otherwise occur. The bullet's core consists mainly of a length of soft steel rod, cut to length during the manufacturing process to give the correct weight. A hollow air space underneath the bullet's thin copper jacket is located ahead of the steel-rod core. The base of the bullet is tapered to reduce vacuum drag (a so-called boat-tail bullet), and a small lead plug is crimped in place in the base of the bullet, ostensibly so that the thin copper alloy jacket material can be stamped in place in the proper tapered shape. The lead plug, however, in combination with that air bubble in the point of the bullet, has the effect of pushing the bullet's center of gravity very far to the rear, and the hollow air space under the point of the bullet makes the bullet's point prone to bending to one side when the bullet strikes anything solid, unbalancing it. Some believed this bullet was designed to tumble in flesh to increase wounding potential.

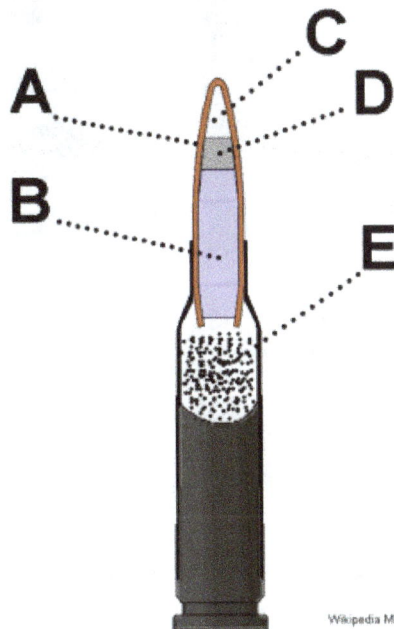

Figure 1-36 Sectional drawing of a cartridge 5.45 x 39mm

A- Projectile jacket   B- Steel core   C- Hollow point
D- Lead inlay   E- Propelling charge

At the time, it was mistakenly believed that yawing and cavitation of projectiles was of major importance in producing tissue damage. Although Dr. Martin Fackler later showed that projectile fragmentation was the key to producing significant wounding effect, this point was unknown to the Soviets when they began development of the new round. This effect was similarly unknown to the non-Soviet alarmists who feared that they had achieved wounding parity with the 5.56 x 45mm NATO round used in the West's M16.

However, the rigidity of the 5.45mm bullet prevents fragmentation and gave it a reputation for being a mediocre stopper. Reports of the 5.45 projectile producing horrific wounds have been repeatedly demonstrated to be false. In his terminal ballistics study using live pigs and ballistic gelatin (1984), Fackler was able to demonstrate that the AK-74, even at close range, did no more damage than a handgun round. The only exception was a hit to the liver, which caused heavy damage due to the stiffness of the organ. All other organs and tissue were too flexible to be severely damaged by the temporary stretch effect.

With the 5.45 mm bullet, the tumbling produced a temporary stretch cavity twice, at 100 and 400 mm of depth, comparable to modern 7.62 x 39mm ammunition and to tungsten penetrator (non-fragmenting) 5.56 x 45mm ammunition. The average width of a human trunk is 15.75-inches/400mm.

Figure 1-37   **Figure 1-38**   **Figure 1-39**   **Figure 1-40**
Ball   Tracer   Blank   Civilian

Caliber, mm	Case	Bullet type	Bullet, wt. Grain	Primer Type	Description
5.45 x 39	Bimetal	Bimetal	52.9	Berdan	Steel Core
5.45 x 39	Bimetal	Tracer	49.8	Berdan	Tracer Bullet
5.45 x 39	Bimetal	Plastic	9.26	Berdan	Plastic blank
5.45 x 39	Bimetal	Bimetal	48	Berdan	Lead Core

5.45 x 39mm 53 grain military ball ammunition

BC: 0.326 G1   CAL: 5.45 mm   WGT: 53 gr

MV: 2950 ft/s   CH: 10 ft

WS: 10 mph   TS: 10 mph

T: 59 °F   PC: 29.92 in Hg   H: 0%   A: 0 ft

SH: 1.5 in   SO: 0 in   ZH: 0 in   LOS: 0°

Range	Drop		Wind		Lead	
(m)	**(in)**	**(moa)**	**(in)**	**(moa)**	**(in)**	**(moa)**
100	3.8	3.3	1.1	1.0	20.6	18.0
200	3.1	1.3	4.8	2.1	43.8	19.1
250	**-0.0**	**-0.0**	**7.7**	**2.7**	**56.5**	**19.7**
300	-5.2	-1.5	11.5	3.3	70.0	20.4
400	-23.3	-5.1	21.8	4.8	99.8	21.8
500	-54.0	-9.4	36.4	6.4	133.9	23.4
600	-101.5	-14.8	56.0	8.2	173.1	25.2
700	-170.9	-21.3	81.3	10.1	217.9	27.2
800	-268.8	-29.3	112.3	12.3	268.4	29.3

5.45 x 39mm Ballistic chart

NOTE: **Minute of Angle (MOA):** The term Minute of Angle, referred to as MOA, is actually a unit of measure dealing with circles found in surveying, navigation, and mathematics. One Minute of Angle is 1/60th of one degree of a circle. A circle has 360 degrees, and there are 21,600 Minutes of Angle in a circle.

If you were to look at a circle which has a radius of 100 yards and project lines out from the center in Minute of Angle increments, you would find that at 100 yards away from the center of the circle the distance between the Minute of Angle lines would be 1.0472 inches.

Over time, one Minute of Angle at 100 yards has been rounded off to one inch and has become a standard unit of measurement for bullet trajectory calculations, comparisons, accuracy levels, and the sighting-in of firearms.

The chart below illustrates the Minute of Angle concept and plots what one, two, and three Minutes of Angle would be at various distances.

One, Two and Three Minute of Angle (MOA) Chart

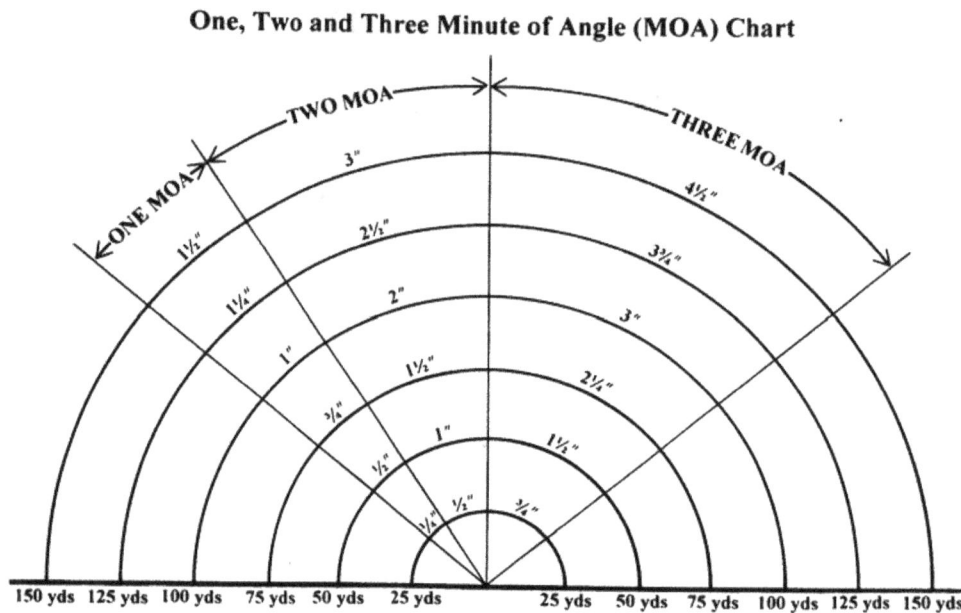

The chart below shows another viewpoint of how Minute of Angle measurements apply to firearms and accuracy. Frequently, a weapon's accuracy is described as being able to fire groups that are less than one Minute of Angle at 100 yards, which would mean that if the shooter fired five rounds at a target 100 yards away and used correct sight alignment, the group would measure less than one inch.

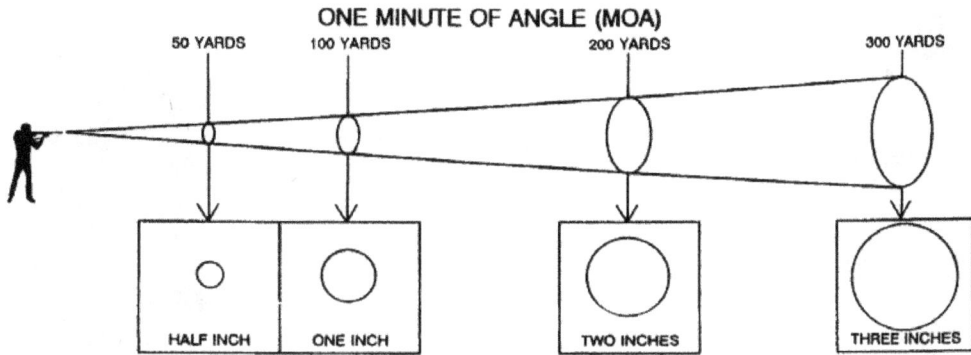

ONE MINUTE OF ANGLE (MOA)

| 50 YARDS | 100 YARDS | 200 YARDS | 300 YARDS |

| HALF INCH | ONE INCH | TWO INCHES | THREE INCHES |

AK/AKM Ammunition Magazines and Drums

The weapon is fed by magazines. Standard magazines are designed to hold 30 rounds for both the AK-47 and AK-74.

AK-47 Magazines

Figure 1-41 30-round plastic magazine

Figure 1-42 30-round metal magazine

Figure 1-43 75-round metal drum

AK-74 Magazines

This section on the AK-74-type magazines has been reprinted with permission from Mark A. Welter of the Shooter Gallery. Mark was willing to allow us to add this to explain better what is out there so if you capture it, you can correctly report it. This section covers all 5.45x39mm magazine types regularly encountered in the United States. Those types rarely or never seen in the United States are listed at the end of this guide under "Exotics." The information presented here is based on detailed examination of Mark's own magazine collection, as well as on material contained in published reference works and input from knowledgeable individuals on The AK Forum and other Internet sites. Photos are copyright Mark Welter unless otherwise noted.

For each magazine type listed are the relative frequency with which it can be found on the open market. These ratings are approximations based on my own experience and research, and are subject to change. For the purposes of this Guide, the following definitions apply:
- **Plentiful** - Large numbers available at any given time in new or used condition from several sources.
- **Very Common** - Large numbers available at any given time in new or used condition from at least one source.
- **Common** - Large numbers frequently available in new or used condition from at least one source.
- **Uncommon** - Occasionally available from domestic or overseas sources. Numbers and condition will vary.
- **Rare** - Limited numbers occasionally available from individual collectors or overseas vendors. Condition will vary.
- **Scarce** - Very limited numbers occasionally available from individual collectors or overseas vendors. Condition will vary.

RUSSIA

Figure 1-44 Russian Izhmash (left) and Tula (right)
30-round BAKELITE

Manufacturers: Izhmash (left) and Tula (right)
Frequency: Uncommon (Izhmash), Rare (Tula)

Description: The first Russian 5.45mm magazine type produced. Constructed from AG-4 phenolic resin (commonly known as "bakelite") with metal lip reinforcement, rear locking lug, and floorplate. Distinctive mottled orange color. Arsenal mark on right side, mold number on left, near bottom of magazine body. Some examples may bear a small white "Made in Russia" sticker. Izhmash produced these magazines for the AK-74 and AKS-74 rifles; Tula produced them for the AKS-74U carbine. This magazine type was officially replaced in the early 1980s, but large numbers are still in front-line service with Russian military forces.

Notes: Similar to E. German 30-round Bakelite, but generally darker in color with more pronounced streaking/mottling. Some of these magazines were painted black, allegedly to help differentiate between the bakelite 5.45 and 7.62 mags when both were simultaneously in widespread use. Examples have been seen with silver ink acceptance stamps applied *over* the black paint, indicating the painting was done at the factory.

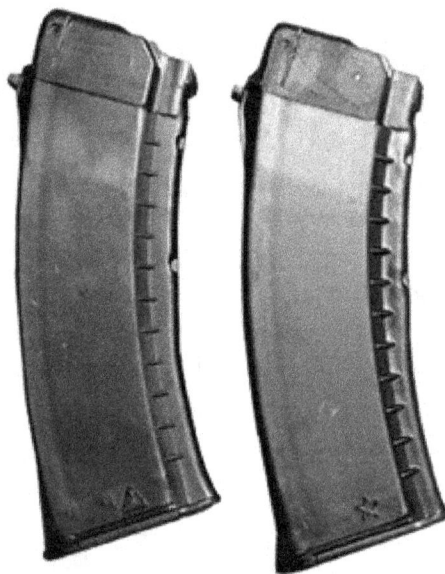

Figure 1-45 Russian Izhmash (left) and Tula (right)

30-round SHINY PLUM
Manufacturers: Izhmash (left) and Tula (right)
Frequency: Uncommon (Izhmash), Rare (Tula)

Description: The second Russian 5.45mm magazine type to be developed. Izhmash produced these magazines for the AK-74 and AKS-74 rifles; Tula produced them for the AKS-74U carbine. Polymer construction with metal lip reinforcement, rear locking lug, and floorplate. Shade varies from maroon to near black; exterior finish can be gloss to semi-gloss. Small horizontal reinforcing ribs run down both sides of the magazine body near the front. Arsenal mark on right side, mold number on left, near bottom of magazine body – mold numbers for this type range up to the low 40s. A black overspray may be present on the top and bottom sections or over the entire magazine; this modification was allegedly done to protect the metal parts from corrosion.

Notes: Similar to Russian (Izhmash) 30-round Matte Plum; some overlap in mold numbers. May be quite difficult to distinguish the two types except under certain lighting conditions. Some examples have been "sanitized" by grinding away the arsenal mark; this action significantly reduces the collector value of the magazine. Very early (single-digit mold number) magazines of this type have been seen with metal followers and floorplate inserts (see pic in Comparison Photos section below). Magazines imported via Bulgaria may contain brown Bulgarian internals.

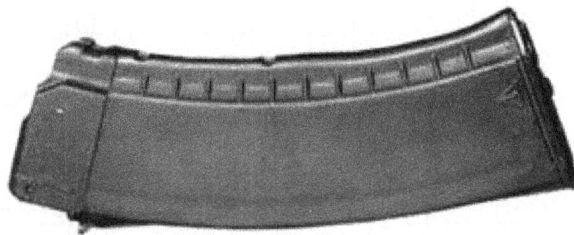

Figure 1-46 Russian Izhmash Matte Plum

30-round MATTE PLUM
Manufacturer: Izhmash
Frequency: Common

Description: The third Russian 5.45mm magazine type produced. Polymer construction with metal lip reinforcement, rear locking lug, and floorplate. Shade varies from maroon to near black, with a non-reflective satin finish. Small horizontal reinforcing ribs run down both sides of the magazine body near the front. Arsenal mark is on right side, mold number is on left, near bottom of magazine body – mold numbers for this type range from the low 40s, up. A black overspray may be present on the top and bottom sections or over the entire magazine; this modification was allegedly done to protect the metal parts from corrosion.

Notes: Similar to Russian (Izhmash) 30-round Shiny Plum; some overlap in mold numbers. May be quite difficult to distinguish the two types except under certain lighting conditions. Some examples have been "sanitized" by grinding away the arsenal mark; this action significantly reduces the collector value of the magazine. Also, magazines imported via Bulgaria may contain brown Bulgarian internals.

Figure 1-47 Russian Izhmash black

30-round TRUE BLACK
Manufacturer: Izhmash
Frequency: Scarce

Description: Current-production magazine for the AK-74M and AK-105. Polymer construction with metal lip reinforcement, rear locking lug, and floorplate. Color is dead black with no purple/maroon undertone; exterior finish is non-reflective satin. Small horizontal reinforcing ribs run down both sides of the magazine body near the front. Arsenal mark on right side, mold number on left, near bottom of magazine body – mold numbers for this type range from high 40s, up.

Notes: Similar to Russian (Izhmash) 30 round Matte Plum; some overlap in mold numbers. May be quite difficult to distinguish between the two types by color alone, except under certain lighting conditions. True Black mags can be identified by the presence of a "4" ink stamp near the front locking lug, where plum mags will show an "M" stamp. Also similar to Bulgarian and Polish 30 round Black Poly types, except for markings. Example shown has been "demilled" by grinding off the feed lips; it was used for demo purposes at the SHOT Show in 2005.

Figure 1-48 Russian 45-round bakelite

45 round BAKELITE
Manufacturer: Molot (Vyatskie Polyany Arsenal)
Frequency: Uncommon

Description: Manufactured for the RPK-74 light machinegun, but usable in all 5.45x39mm caliber AK rifles and carbines. Constructed from AG-4 phenolic resin (commonly known as "bakelite") with metal lip reinforcement, rear locking lug, and floorplate. Distinctive mottled orange color. Arsenal mark on right side, mold number on left, near bottom of magazine body. Approximately 1/3 longer than a 30-round magazine.

Notes: Identical to Bulgarian 45- round Bakelite, except for the presence of Molot arsenal mark. Some examples have been "sanitized" by grinding away the arsenal mark; this action significantly reduces the collector value of the magazine.

Figure 1-49 Russian 45-round ribbed plum

45-round RIBBED PLUM
Manufacturer: Molot (Vyatskie Polyany Arsenal)
Frequency: Scarce

Description: Manufactured for the later-model RPK-74 light machinegun, but usable in all 5.45x39mm caliber AK rifles and carbines. Polymer construction with metal lip reinforcement, rear locking lug, and floorplate. Color is dark plum with black overspray at top and bottom; non-reflective satin finish. Large horizontal reinforcing ribs run down both sides of the magazine body and span almost the entire width. Arsenal mark on right side, mold number on left, at bottom rear corner of magazine body. Approximately 1/3 longer than a 30-round magazine.

Figure 1-50 Russian 10-round ribbed black for VEPR

10-round RIBBED BLACK (VEPR)
Manufacturer: Molot (Vyatskie Polyany Arsenal)
Frequency: Scarce

Description: Built for the export-model 5.45x39mm "VEPR" hunting rifle but capable of being used in other 5.45x39 caliber AK rifles and carbines, this magazine is largely similar in design and construction to the 45-round ribbed plum and black RPK-74 magazines described elsewhere in this Guide. Features include polymer construction with metal lip reinforcement, rear locking lug, and floorplate, and large horizontal reinforcing ribs running down both sides of the magazine body and spanning almost the entire width. Color is dead black with a smooth, semi-reflective finish. Markings include Molot company logo (as opposed to the star-in-shield arsenal mark) on right side of magazine body and large "5,45" caliber designation on left side, both in the lower rear corner. A small mold number appears on the left side, forward of the caliber marking. Floorplate is of a recessed or internal design, differing from all other 5.45mm Kalashnikov magazines. Magazine body has rounded edge at bottom rear rather than the slight outward flare found on other polymer types.

Notes: It is unclear how many of these magazines are in the US or how they got here, as the sole American importer of the VEPR line did not bring them in, opting instead to provide 30-round Bulgarian or East German AK-74 magazines with their rifles. The Molot web site also lists a 5 round magazine for the 5.45 VEPR; it is assumed to be similar.

BULGARIA

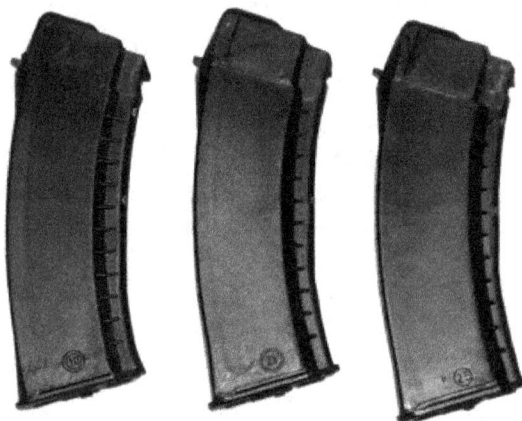

Figure 1-51 Bulgarian Black Poly

30-round BLACK POLY
Manufacturers: Arsenal Inc., NITI Kazanlak and Optico-Electron
Frequency: Plentiful (Arsenal Inc. Code 10), Common (NITI Kazanlak Code 21) Uncommon (Optico-Electron Code 25)

Description: Probably the 5.45mm magazine type most frequently encountered in the US. Construction closely follows the Russian design -- polymer body with small horizontal reinforcing ribs down both sides near the front, and metal lip reinforcement, rear locking lug and floorplate. Color is dead black with a non-reflective matte finish.

Notes: Similar to Russian True Black and Polish Black Poly types, except for markings. NITI Kazanlak Code 21 magazines are frequently encountered with brown replacement part followers and floorplate inserts. Optico-Electron Code 25 magazines appear to be constructed from a harder type of polymer with a much smoother texture than Arsenal Code 10 or NITI Kazanlak Code 21 magazines. NITI (Bulgarian acronym for "Science, Research & Technology Engineering") Kazanlak was the former research & development branch of Arsenal Bulgaria and became a separate state-owned entity when Arsenal became a private corporation.

Figure 1-52 Bulgarian 30-round plum and green

30-round PLUM & O.D. GREEN POLY
Manufacturer: Arsenal Inc.
Frequency: Uncommon

Description: In late 2006, K-VAR Corporation (a US affiliate of Arsenal Inc.) commissioned Arsenal to produce a run of plum and OD green AK-74 magazines for the US commercial market. Except for the colors, these magazines are identical to the Code 10 black polymer type described above. The plum and OD colors match the polymer stock sets offered by K-VAR.

Notes: It is unknown how many of these colored magazines were or will be produced. Because of this lack of knowledge and because K-VAR is the sole importer, the frequency value of "Uncommon" was assigned.

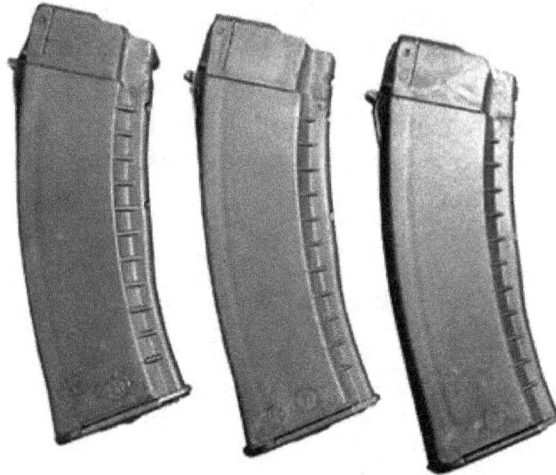

Figure 1-53 Bulgarian 30-round brown variations

30-ond BROWN/SADDLE TAN/FIREBRICK RED POLY
Manufacturer: NITI Kazanlak (Brown/Saddle Tan/Firebrick Red) and Optico-Electron (Firebrick Red only)
Frequency: Very Common (NITI Kazanlak Code 21 Brown), Uncommon (NITI Kazanlak Code 21 Saddle Tan & Firebrick Red), Scarce (Optico-Electron Code 25 Firebrick Red)

Description: Construction is identical to the Black Poly magazines described previously. It is unknown whether the color nomenclature is official, or simply made up by US vendors/consumers in an effort to describe the variations better (that is, they could all be considered "brown" by the manufacturer). Whichever the case, all three colors show wide ranges: Brown can run from dark chocolate to a lighter mocha; Saddle Tan can run from medium brown to burnt orange, and Firebrick Red can be anything from reddish-brown to maroon. Complicating matters even more is that the colors can appear differently as lighting conditions change.

Notes: All three colors commonly have black ink splotches on the magazine body, and may be encountered with brown replacement part followers and floorplate inserts. Optico-Electron Code 25 magazines appear to be constructed from a harder type of polymer with a much smoother texture than the NITI Kazanlak Code 21 magazines. NITI (Bulgarian acronym for "Science, Research & Technology Engineering") Kazanlak was the former research & development branch of Arsenal Bulgaria and became a separate state-owned entity when Arsenal became a private corporation.

Figure 1-54 Bulgarian 30-round plum poly

30-round PLUM POLY
Manufacturers: NITI Kazanlak
Frequency: Scarce

Description: A previously unknown color variation first identified in 2007; individual magazines can vary from dark/violet (left) to light/purple (right). Construction and physical features are identical to other Bulgarian Code 21 magazines. These are Bulgarian military surplus and are not related to the previously described Code 10 plum magazines produced by Arsenal Inc. for K-VAR. The Code 10 magazines are a much lighter and browner shade of plum, being specifically color-matched to K-VAR's US-made plum furniture sets (see comparison photos).

Notes: Generally similar to Russian Matte Plum type, except for markings. Actual shade may not be apparent under certain lighting conditions. May be encountered with brown replacement part followers and/or floorplate inserts. NITI (Bulgarian acronym for "Science, Research & Technology Engineering") Kazanlak was the former research & development branch of Arsenal Bulgaria and became a separate state-owned entity when Arsenal became a private corporation.

Figure 1-55 Bulgarian 45-round bakelite

45-round BAKELITE
Manufacturer: Unknown; probably Molot
Frequency: Common

Description: Manufactured for the RPK-74 light machinegun, but usable in all 5.45x39mm caliber AK rifles and carbines. Constructed from AG-4 phenolic resin (commonly known as "bakelite") with metal lip reinforcement, rear locking lug and floorplate. Distinctive mottled orange color. Empty disc on right side, mold number on left, near bottom of magazine body. Approximately 1/3 longer than a 30-round magazine.

Notes: Identical to Russian 45-round Bakelite except for the absence of Molot arsenal mark; Bulgarian RPK-74 magazines were most likely produced by Molot in Russia under contract. These are more commonly encountered and bring far lower prices than the arsenal-marked Russian equivalent.

Figure 1-56 Bulgarian 45-round black waffle

45-round BLACK WAFFLE
Manufacturer: Arsenal Inc.
Frequency: Uncommon

Description: Polymer construction with metal lip reinforcement, rear locking lug and floorplate. Features five vertical reinforcement ribs at the top and bottom of the magazine, with the 2nd and 4th ribs running the full length of the mag body. These intersect with horizontal ribs along the magazine's midsection, creating a distinctive "waffle" pattern similar to that found in Arsenal's 7.62x39mm and 5.56x45mm AK magazines. The horizontal ribs wrap around to the spine of the magazine, but not to the front. Color is dead black with a slightly reflective textured finish. Arsenal mark appears on the upper right side of the magazine, just above the first horizontal rib. Approximately 1/3 longer than a 30-round magazine.

Notes: First appearing in March 2008, these magazines were produced at K-VAR's request specifically for the US commercial market, as had previously been done with the plum and OD green 30-round magazines (see above). Because it is unknown how many of these magazines were or will be manufactured, and because K-VAR is the sole importer, the frequency value of "Uncommon" was assigned.

POLAND

Figure 1-57 Polish 30-round steel

30-round STEEL
Manufacturer: Lucznik (Radom)
Frequency: Common

Description: Manufactured for the wz.88 "Tantal" assault rifle, the Polish equivalent to the AK-74. All-steel construction with large vertical ribs and smaller interlocking horizontal ribs on the sides of the body, and a prominent dorsal spine. Semi-gloss, slightly rough black finish (painted). No arsenal logo or proof marks evident.

Notes: Generally similar in construction and appearance to Eastern Bloc AKM 7.62x39mm magazines, but with a straighter profile. Nearly identical to the less common Romanian 30-round 5.45 magazine, except for slight differences in the spine, feed lip reinforcement area, and finish.

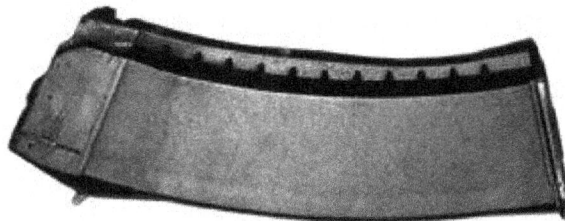

Figure 1-58 Polish 30-round black poly

30-round BLACK POLY
Manufacturer: Lucznik (Radom)
Frequency: Uncommon

Description: Manufactured for the wz.88 "Tantal" assault rifle, the Polish equivalent to the AK-74. Construction closely follows the Russian design -- polymer body with small horizontal reinforcing ribs down both sides near the front, and metal lip reinforcement, rear locking lug and floorplate. Color is dead black with a slightly reflective finish. Mold number appears on the left side of the magazine body near the bottom. No arsenal mark is present, though a small diamond-shaped proof stamp may be found on the spine just above the floorplate.

Notes: This is the early type Tantal magazine; later versions are marked with the caliber designation and show other minor differences (see below). Because they are a relatively obscure type and lack markings save for the mold number, these early Tantal magazines are often misrepresented by sellers as Bulgarian, Russian or East German.

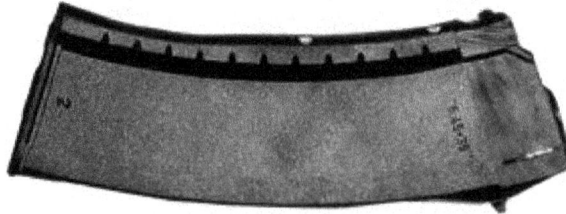

Figure 1-59 Polish 30-round black poly with caliber identification

30-round BLACK POLY w/ CALIBER MARKING
Manufacturer: Lucznik (Radom)
Frequency: Uncommon

Description: Manufactured for the wz.88 "Tantal" assault rifle, the Polish equivalent to the AK-74. Construction closely follows the Russian design - polymer body with small horizontal reinforcing ribs down both sides near the front, and metal lip reinforcement, rear locking lug and floorplate. Color is dead black with a frosted/textured finish. Mold number appears on the left side of the magazine body near the bottom, and caliber designation "5,45x39" appears on the left side roughly parallel to the rear locking lug. No arsenal mark is present.

Notes: This is the later type Tantal magazine, marked with the caliber to distinguish it from the nearly identical wz.89/96 magazine (which is marked "5,56x45"). The caliber-marked Tantal magazines also lack the proof mark and drain hole found on the spine of the earlier types.

ROMANIA

Figure 1-60 Romanian 5-round steel

5-round STEEL
Manufacturer: Cugir Arsenal
Frequency: Rare

Description: Created for the US commercial market during the "Assault Weapons Ban" era and supplied with the CUR-2, the first type of 5.45x39mm rifle imported by Century Arms International in the mid-1990s. These appear to have been fabricated by cutting down a 30-round steel magazine. When Century Arms transitioned from importing the thumbhole-stocked, all-Romanian CUR-2 to the pistol-gripped, 922(r) compliant SAR-2 in the late 1990s, the 5rd magazine was discontinued in favor of a 10-round steel magazine (see below). 5-round steel magazines of this type can occasionally be found for sale on the secondhand market and retain some value as curiosities and collectors' items. Their short length also makes them convenient when shooting from a bench rest.

Figure 1-61 Romanian 10-round steel

10-round STEEL
Manufacturer: Cugir Arsenal
Frequency: Uncommon

Description: Created for the US commercial market during the "Assault Weapons Ban" era and supplied with the SAR-2 5.45x39mm rifles imported by Century Arms International in the late 1990s and early 2000s. These appear to have been fabricated by cutting down a 30-round steel magazine of the type described below. Century Arms stopped furnishing the 10rd magazines with their rifles in about 2002 (switching to East German 30-round bakelites, then to Bulgarian 30-round polymer types), and the sunset of the AWB in 2004 largely eliminated demand for them in the US. They can occasionally be found for sale on the secondhand market, and retain some value as curiosities and collectors' items. Their short length also makes them convenient when shooting from a bench rest.

Figure 1-62 Romanian 30-round steel

30-round STEEL
Manufacturer: Cugir Arsenal
Frequency: Uncommon

Description: All-steel construction with large vertical ribs and smaller interlocking horizontal ribs on the sides of the body, and a prominent dorsal spine. Semi-gloss, smooth black finish (blued). A small chevron or arrowhead shape and other proof marks may be present on the dorsal spine.

Notes: Generally similar in construction and appearance to Eastern Bloc AKM 7.62x39mm magazines, but with a straighter profile. Nearly identical to the more common Polish Tantal 30-round steel magazine, except for slight differences in the spine, feed lip reinforcement area, and finish.

Figure 1-63 Romanian 40-round steel

40-round STEEL
Manufacturer: Cugir Arsenal
Frequency: Scarce

Description: Intended for use with the Romanian RPK-74 light machinegun, but compatible with all 5.45x39mm caliber AK rifles and carbines. Construction, finish, and identifying features are identical to the 30-round magazine described above, with the RPK magazine being about 25% longer.

Notes: Generally similar to the Eastern Bloc RPK 7.62x39mm 40-round magazine, but much straighter in profile.

EAST GERMANY

Figure 1-64 East German 30-round Bakelite

30-round BAKELITE
Manufacturer: Unknown, but likely Ernst Thaelmann VEB
Frequency: Plentiful

Description: Second most common type of 5.45 magazine encountered in the United States; huge numbers of these were released into the surplus market after the reunification of Germany in the early 1990s, and new-condition examples could be had for as little as $3.00 apiece at one point. In recent years, supplies have tightened, and prices have gone up, but there are still plenty of these magazines to be had, and they are still used as OEM magazines by at least two US manufacturers/importers. Constructed from AG-4 phenolic resin (commonly known as "bakelite") with metal lip reinforcement, rear locking lug and floorplate. Distinctive orange color. Mold number on right side near bottom of magazine body; no arsenal mark present. Some examples may bear a small white "Made in Germany" sticker.

Notes: Similar to Russian 30-round Bakelites, but generally lighter in color with less pronounced streaking/mottling. Robinson Armament uses East German Bakelites coated in a textured black finish as OEM magazines for their VEPR rifles; beware of these being misrepresented on the secondhand market. Lack of reinforcement ribs and arsenal marks and the presence of the mold number on the right side rather than the left will distinguish these black EG Bakelites from the Bulgarian, Russian, and Polish polymer mags. Also, EG Bakelites modified by Century Arms for use with .223/5.56x45mm rifles can be distinguished by a band of black paint around the top of the magazine and a large white identification sticker on the magazine body.

COMPARISON PHOTOS

Figure 1-65 Relative size of 30-, 40- and 45-round 5.45x39mm Kalashnikov magazines

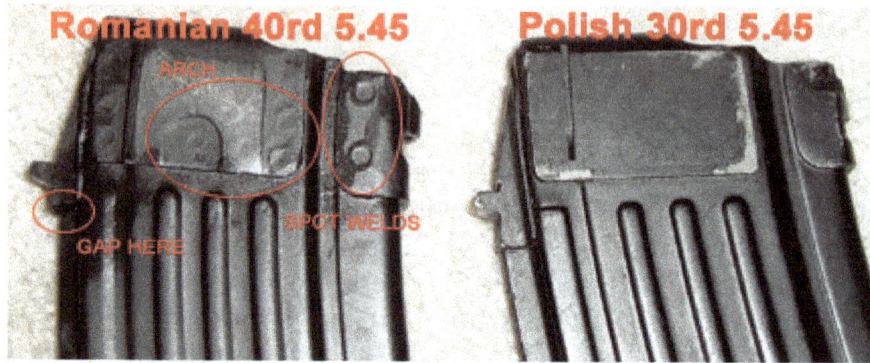

Figure 1-66 Romanian and Polish steel mags, with differences highlighted

Figure 1-67 Bulgarian magazine colors: *(left to right)* **Black, Brown, Saddle Tan, Firebrick Red, Plum**

Figure 1-68 45-round Bakelite mags; Russian w/Molot arsenal mark (left) and Bulgarian w/ empty disc (right)

Figure 1-69 Very early Izhmash plum magazines showing metal (left) and polymer (right) followers. *Photo courtesy of "MT-LB" on The AK Forum.*

Figure 1-70 Plum polymer mags: *(left to right)* **Izhmash matte, Izhmash shiny, Tula shiny, Bulgarian Code 21**

Figure 1-71 Bulgarian Code 21 (left) and Code 10 (right) plum magazines

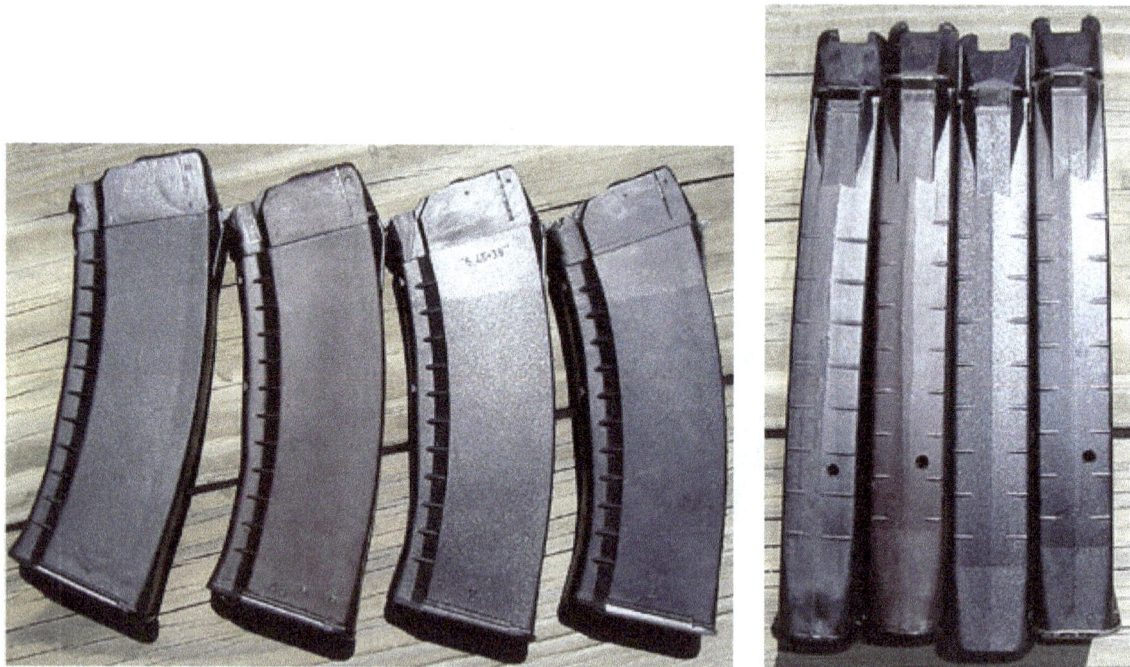

Figures 1-72a and 1-72b Polymer mags compared: *(left to right)* **Bulgarian Code 10, Izhmash matte plum, Polish (late), and Polish (early)**

Figure 1-73 RPK-74 magazines: *(left to right)* **Bulgarian bakelite, Russian (Molot) bakelite, Russian (Molot) plum, Bulgarian Code 10 waffle, Romanian steel**

MAGAZINE MARKINGS

Figures 1-74a-c Bulgarian Arsenal Marks - *(left to right)* **Arsenal Inc. Code 10, NITI Kazanlak Code 21, Optico Electron Code 25**

Figures 1-75a-d Russian Arsenal Marks - *(top left to bottom right)* **Izhmash large/small, Tula, and Molot**

Figures 1-76a-d Mold Numbers - *(top left to bottom right)* **Bulgarian, East German, Polish, and Russian**

Russian Acceptance Stamps/Proof Marks

Figures 1-77a-h Russian acceptance stamps/proof marks

Bulgarian Acceptance Stamps/Proof Marks

Figures 1-78a-c Bulgarian acceptance stamps/proof marks

Romanian Proof Marks - *(left to right)* Chevron, "3", "Y"

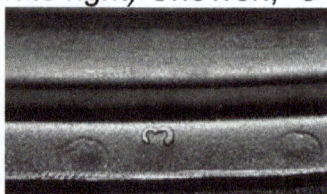

Figure 1-79 Romanian acceptance stamp/proof marks

EXOTICS

Figure 1-80 East German 30- and 45-round magazine comparison

EAST GERMAN 45-round BAKELITE

Generally similar to the Bulgarian/Russian design, but having the mold number on the right side and nothing on the left, in the manner of the 30-round magazines from the same country. To my knowledge, none have ever been imported into the U.S. for sale, though a few examples may have entered mixed in with the more common Bulgarian magazines. *(Photo courtesy of "The_Boy_Swift" on The AK Forum; East German mag on left, Molot mag on right)*

Figure 1-81 Chinese 30-round steel AK-74 magazine

CHINESE 30-round

Description: Norinco had plans to market a semi-auto AK-74 in the United States, but only a handful of sales samples (3 confirmed, possibly others) made it in before the Assault Weapons Ban of 1994 was enacted. This legislation, along with import restrictions on "non-sporting" arms from China, curtailed any further plans for Chinese AK-74s. The Chinese 5.45x39mm magazines are steel and of a "flatback" design, lacking the dorsal spine found on the Polish and Romanian types. In November of 2006, one of these mags was sold for $180 by an individual in Switzerland on an AK-related Internet forum. I have heard from a knowledgeable source that a small number had previously made it into the US in a similar manner, and that there were also a few sales samples in-country prior to the ban. This makes the Chinese 30-round the only "exotic" 5.45x39mm magazine that is even *remotely* obtainable. *(Photo courtesy of "AD 1" on The AK Forum)*

Figure 1-82 North Korean 30-round steel magazine

NORTH KOREAN 30-round

Description: Very little is known about the North Korean AK-74 variant, save for what can be gleaned from propaganda photos and a couple of badly worn/corroded/damaged examples that have been recovered. It appears to use a steel 30 round magazine very similar to the Chinese pattern. *(Photo courtesy of Rob Stott)*

Figure 4-83 Pakistan 30-round polymer

PAKISTANI "KHYBER PASS" 30-round POLYMER

Description: Apparently a Pakistani near-clone of the Russian polymer 30-round magazine, fabricated by the provincial gunsmiths of the Afghanistan/Pakistan border regions as opposed to a state arsenal. These are constructed from red/orange polymer material (not bakelite), and feature reinforcing ribs, floorplates, and metal locking lugs nearly identical to the Russian style; there is even a reproduction of the Izhmash "arrow-in-triangle" arsenal mark on the bottom right side of the magazine body. The "Khyber Pass" magazines can be distinguished from genuine Izhmash magazines by the color and texture of the magazine body, as well as a unique (presumably Pakistani) arsenal mark in place of the mold number on the lower left side of the magazine body. This marking appears to be a triangular design featuring the letters "S G A" in stylized script. Magazines of this type have been seen alongside Pakistani built/modified AK-74-type rifles at the Royal Armory in England, and more recently, a few have been brought back by US troops returning from deployments to Iraq and Afghanistan. *(Photos courtesy of MachinegunBooks.com)*

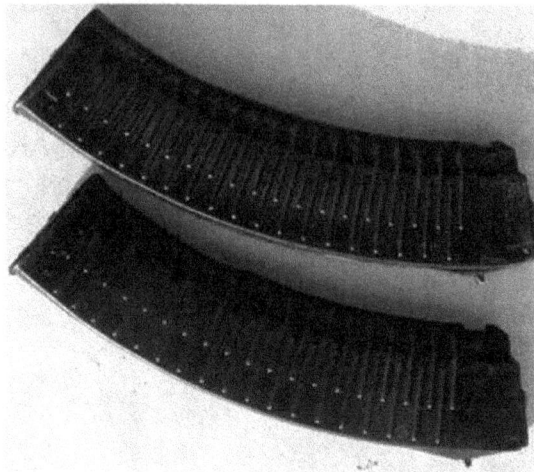

Figure 1-84 Russian 45-round ribbed plum and ribbed black

RUSSIAN 45-round RIBBED "TRUE BLACK"

Current production magazine for the RPK-74M light machinegun. Identical to the 45-round Ribbed Plum type described previously, but dead black in color. This type is virtually unknown outside of Russia due to that country's restrictions on export and civilian ownership of military items. An extremely small number leaked into the European market, and from there, at least one has made it into the hands of a collector in the United States. *(Photo courtesy of Rob Stott; 45-round Ribbed Plum mag on top, 45 round True Black mag on bottom)*

Figure 1-85 Russian 20-round bakelite

RUSSIAN 20-round BAKELITE

Description: The only evidence of this magazine's existence comes from a St. Petersburg museum exhibit *(left; photo courtesy of Rob Stott)*, and it is unlikely the type was produced in quantities beyond a few prototypes. The intent was probably to provide a shorter magazine for the AKS-74U carbine for use by vehicle crews and in other applications requiring maximum compactness and maneuverability. The shorter length is also handy when shooting off a bench, so I had several of my East German 30-round bakelite mags cut down and reassembled into 20-round magazines *(right)* similar to the one shown in the museum photo.

Figure 1-86 Russian 60-round quad stack

RUSSIAN 60-round QUAD STACK

Description: The origins of this unusual polymer magazine are unclear, but it seems reasonable to assume it was intended for use with the RPK-74 light machinegun. Essentially two 30-round magazines fused together, the quad stack features "blown out" sides tapering down to a standard double-column feed neck, with dual springs and followers inside. Pictures and engineering drawings of this magazine have been circulating around the Internet for some time. Rarely seen even in Russia, these may not have progressed beyond the prototype stage. None were ever imported into the US, though at least a couple individuals have endeavored to build one of their own, with varying degrees of success. *(Photo courtesy of Joe Ancona and Jason Jeffers)*

Figure 1-87 RPK-74 pan drum magazine

RUSSIAN RPK-74 PAN DRUM

Description: This experimental drum magazine for the RPK-74 locks into the gun in the manner of a normal 30-round magazine, but the drum body is oriented almost parallel to the barrel (rather than vertically or angled slightly forward as with the 7.62x39mm drums). Polymer construction; capacity is said to be 100 rounds. A few photos have been widely circulated, and urban legend has it that one of the prototypes sold on the Internet for around $3500. *(Photo found on the Internet; shows drum mounted to a PU-1 experimental light machine gun, which could be fed from belts or magazines)*

AK74 Ammunition Packaging

AK-47/AKM Ammunition Packaging - Typical packaging in two 820-round metal cans in a wooden case for a total of 1640 rounds. The individual rounds will be packaged in paper in quantities of 20 rounds.

AK-74 Ammunition Packaging - Typical packaging in two 1080-round metal cans in a wooden case for a total of 2160 rounds. The individual rounds will be packaged in paper in quantities of 30 rounds.

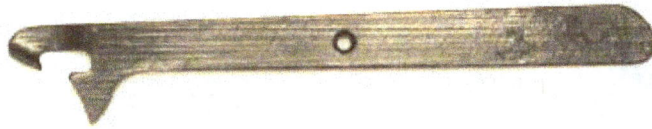

Figure 1-88 Metal ammunition can opener

Metal can opener used to open the sardine-style metal cans; one opener will be in each wooden crate that contains the two metal ammo cans. Without it, opening the cans is quite an adventure; we have used Leatherman tool, chisels, and bayonets. If using a bayonet or other non-designed can opener, be careful not to beat a bayonet tip into one of the primers.

Section 2

Maintenance

Clearing the AK style rifle

Figure 2-1 Safety/selector lever (on SAFE)

A. Ensure the rifle is on safe. At all time during the clearing, you must remain aware to not touch the trigger and keep the muzzle pointed in a safe direction (Figure 2-1).

Figure 2-2a and 2-2b Removing the magazine

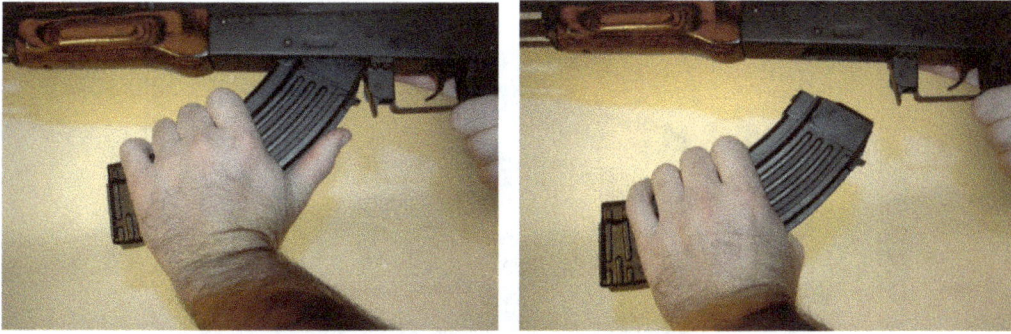

Figure 2-2c and 2-2d Removing the magazine

B. Remove the magazine by pressing the magazine catch towards the rear of the magazine and rock the magazine forward to release it. Place the magazine down or in a pouch.

Figure 2-3 Removing any loaded ammunition from chamber

C. Place the rifle on FIRE (semi-automatic or automatic) and pull the charging handle to the rear and hold it back. Observe the round extracting and ejecting from the ejection port; do not attempt to retain the round (Figure 2-3).

Figure 2-4 Inspection of the chamber

D. Visually observe that there is no magazine in the rifle and no round in the chamber; physically check with your finger in low-light conditions (Figure 2-4).

Figure 2-5 Safety/selector lever (on SAFE)

E. Return the rifle's safety lever to the SAFE position (top position) (Figure 2-5).

Disassembling the AK

To insure the proper function of the AKM it is necessary to disassemble the weapon to inspect and clean the internal components. The names of the parts should be learned through practice in disassembling and reassembling to enhance operator competence. Generally the parts are named for the functions they perform, i.e., the trigger guard guards the trigger, the charging handle is used to charge the weapon, etc.

AK type rifle completely disassembled and ready for cleaning and inspection.

Figure 2-6 Disassembled AK rifle

When the operator begins to disassemble the weapon, it should be done in the following order:

To begin the disassembly-

1. First clear the weapon as per the above description, depending on the weapon's condition.

2. Place the weapon on a flat, clean surface with the muzzle oriented in a safe direction.

Figure 2-7 Depressing the carrier spring button

3. Grasp the weapon by the buttstock, and with your free hand, depress the receiver cover latch button (Figure 2-7).

Figure 2-8 Removing the receiver cover

4. Lift off the receiver cover and set it aside with room to continue the disassembly progressively (Figure 2-8).

Figure 2-9a Depressing the carrier spring button

Figure 2-9b Removing the carrier spring button

5. Depress the carrier spring by pushing it towards the muzzle and lift it out (Figure 2-9a and 2-9b).

Figure 2-10a Removing the bolt carrier

Figure 2-10b Removing the bolt carrier

6. Place the safety selector on one of the lower positions and pull back the bolt to the rear and lift the bolt carrier/gas piston assembly out of the receiver. Watch the bolt! It is loose and with a turn will fall out (Figure 2-10a and 2-10b).

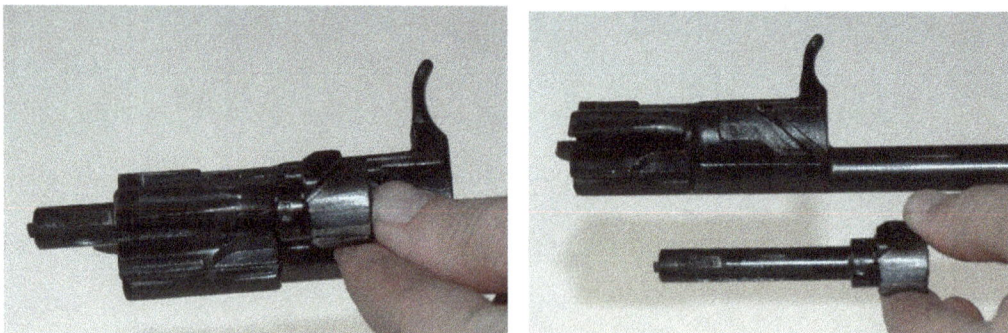

Figure 2-11 Removing the bolt from the carrier

7. Remove it by turning it until the locking tab is clear and you can slide it forward and free (Figure 2-11).

Figure 2-12 Lifting the gas tube retaining lever

8. Finally, with the gas piston cover removed, lift the locking lever on the right side of the gas block up by rotating up towards the muzzle; do not force this (Figure 2-12).

Figure 2-13a and 2-13b Use the cleaning kit storage tube to release this lever; it has a slot in it designed to give you more leverage.

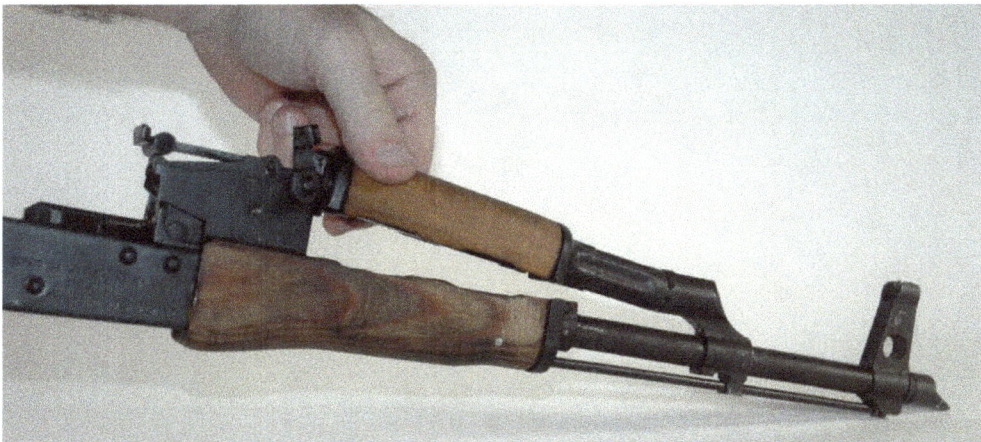

Figure 2-14 Removing the upper handguard/gas tube

9. The gas tube/upper handguard assembly will be loose now, and you can move it upward and off the gun (Figure 2-14).

10. The rifle is now ready for cleaning and inspection.

Cleaning and Lubrication

The AKM is a very dependable rifle, but periodic cleaning is advised to insure functionality. Clean the weapon as often as the situation dictates and the environment necessitates.

Keep the weapon free of dirt and dust as much as possible; use a muzzle cap or tape to keep them from the bore. Depending on the operating environment, keep lubricant only on metal-to-metal moving parts and use paint brushes to clean dust and dirt off of and out of the weapon.

Do not clean the inside of the gas piston cover unless you have fired blanks or it is excessively sluggish induced by carbon build-up. Do not put lubricants in the gas piston cover.

In hot and humid climates, inspect the weapon often for signs of rust. Keep the weapon free of moisture and keep a fine coat of lubricating oil on the metal surfaces. If the weapon is exposed to salt air, high humidity, or water, then clean and oil the weapon entirely as often as needed to keep it serviceable.

In hot and dry climates such as deserts, keep the weapon lubricated only on metal-to-metal moving parts and use paint brushes to clean dust and dirt off of and out of the weapon. Keeping the weapon free of unneeded oil will prevent sand and dust from collecting in the receiver and bore.

Keep your ammunition in containers when not in use and clean off the cartridges as necessary.

Clean the barrel with the cleaning rod that is stored under the barrel and the brushes and jags stored in the hollow section of the buttstock. Use solvent-lubricated brass brushes to break up carbon in the bore, and then use a solvent-covered patch to push the carbon out and a then dry patch until it is clean. The bores are chrome lined, so they clean up easily. Keep spare barrels clean by taping the chamber and muzzle, storing them in the spare barrel bags, and inspecting them regularly. A bore snake is a great bore-cleaning product to do this as the barrel is clean with one pass of the bore snake.

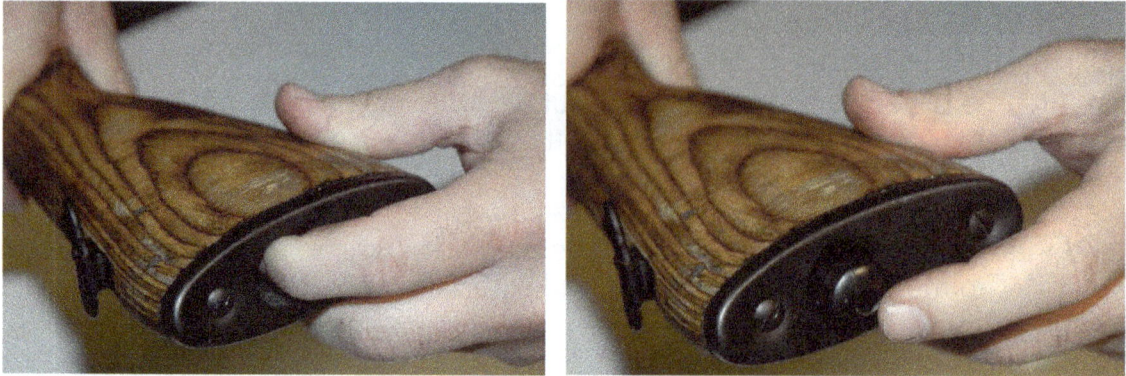

Figure 2-15 Removing the cleaning accessories storage tube

Depress the spring-loaded cover on the butt plate of the stock and allow the tube of cleaning accessories to be pushed out by its spring on wooden stock rifles.

Cleaning Tube and Accessories

Figure 2-16 Cap removed from cleaning accessories storage tube

Figure 2-17 Photo of cleaning accessories in the storage tube

1- Metal storage tube - used as a handle for cleaning rod and combination tool
2- Combination tool - used to scrape carbon, use as a front sight elevation tool and punch pin for disassembling the bolt
3- Nylon-bristled brush to attach to the cleaning rod sections
4- Steel patch jag to attach to the end of the cleaning rod sections
5- Metal storage tube cap - used as a cleaning rod guide

Figure 2-18 Example of the assembled rod with cap and tube used.

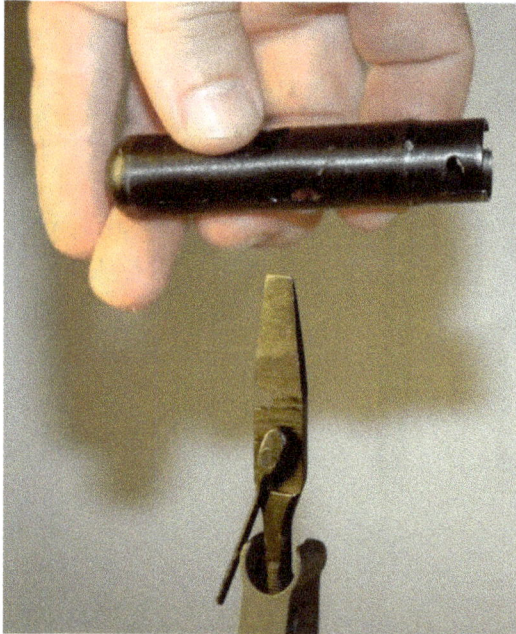

Figure 2-19a   **Figure 2-19b**
Example using the combo tool and tube to adjust elevation

Figure 2-20 Cleaning rod section is stored under the barrel of the weapon.

To remove the cleaning rod section, just pull down on the end of the rod and pull forward.

Bolt Disassembly

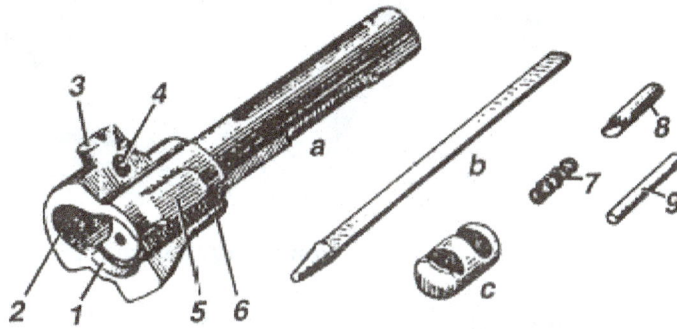

Figure 2-21 Parts of the Bolt

1- Recess for bottom of the case
2- Extractor slot
3- Guide lug
4- Extractor pin hole
5- Locking lug

6- Longitudinal slot for ejector lug
7- Extractor spring
8- Extractor pin
9- Firing pin retaining pin

To disassemble the bolt

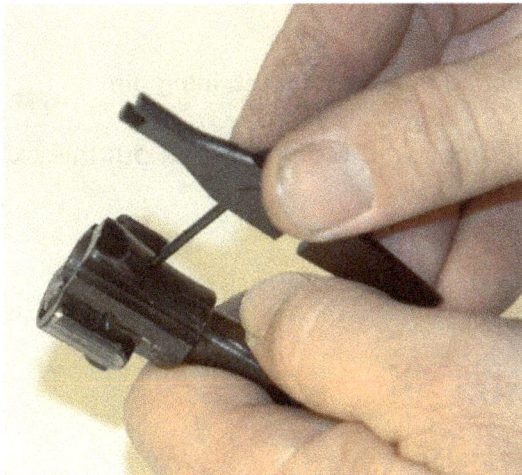

| **Figure 2-22a** | **Figure 2-22b** |

Removing the firing pin retaining pin

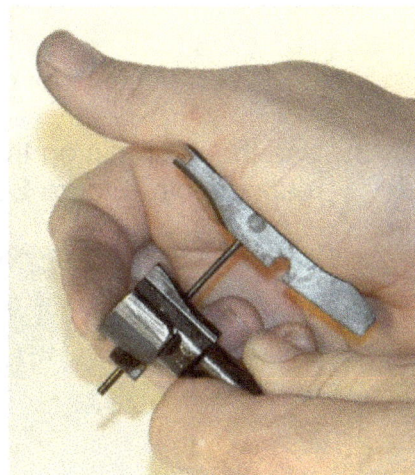

1. Use the push pin on the combination tool to press out the firing pin retaining pin (Figures 2-22a and 2-22b).

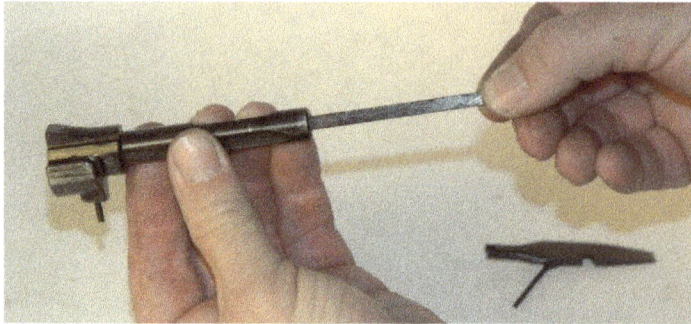

Figure 2-23 Removing the firing pin

2. Remove the firing pin from the rear of the bolt (Figure 2-23).

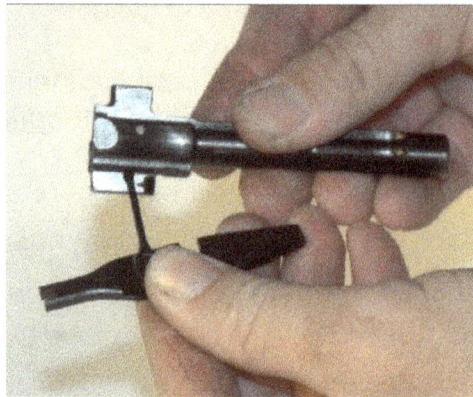

Figure 2-24 Locating the extractor retaining pin

3. Use the push pin on the combination tool to press out the extractor retaining pin (Figure 2-24).

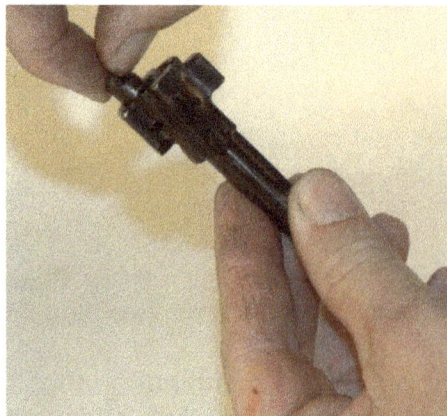

Figure 2-25 Removing extractor and extractor spring

4. Remove the extractor and extractor spring (Figure 2-25).

To reassemble the bolt, reverse the process after inspecting for damage.

Lubrication

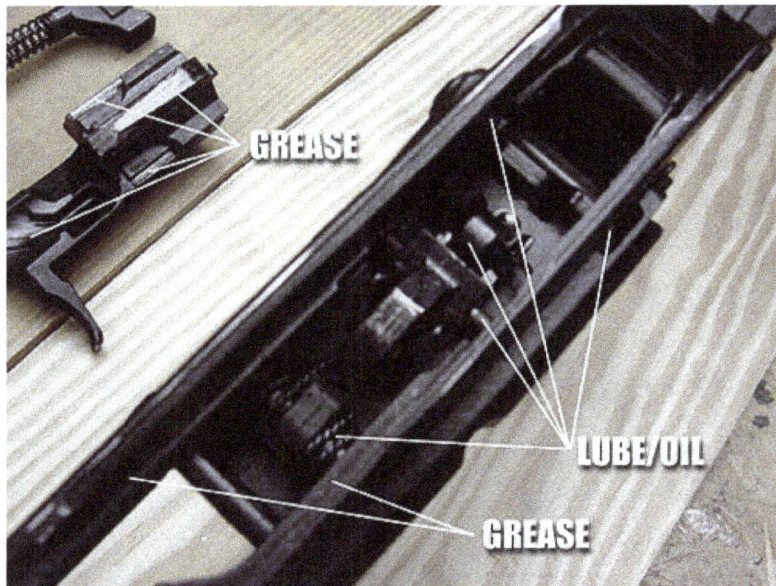

Figure 2-26 Lubrication points

Lube all operating parts. Inside the receiver, go ahead and coat the metal in a light film of CLP or light machine/gun oil. Some type of grease can be used on the metal to metal (shiny spots) to allow the rifle to operate smoothly (Figure 2-26).

Protection
Use a type of Cleaner/Lubricant/Protectant (CLP). When not available some prefer motor oil, automatic transmission fluid, or light gun oil. With a rag, wipe down all exposed metal with CLP, interior and exterior, parkerized, blued, or otherwise. A slight film is all that is required to protect the gun. A new product called Strike-Hold has been developed and works very will for replacement of the standard types of CLP. Strike-Hold is a fast acting penetrating cleaner that immediately cuts through dirt, rust, carbon, and scale to quickly get into parts that have become frozen by or encrusted with corrosion and oxidation. This product provides a long-lasting dry lubricant, which reduces friction and *will not build up or become brittle*. As a demoisturant, Strike-Hold helps dry out wet electrical gears and other water sensitive parts. As a protectant, this product provides a shield-like film against the effects of moisture and corrosion, even against salt water, and actually REPELS SAND, DIRT AND DUST.

How to Disassemble an AK47/74 Magazine

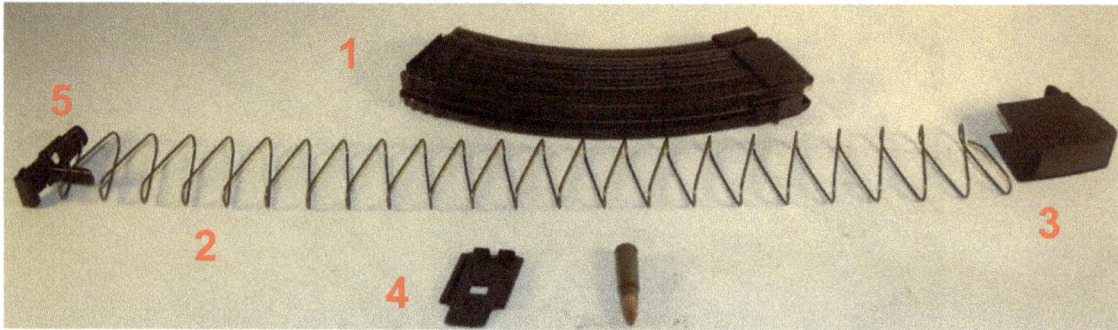

Figure 2-27 Parts of a typical 30 round AK magazine

1- Magazine body
2- Spring
3- Follower

4- Magazine floor plate
5- Retainer plate

To disassemble the magazine, ensure the magazine is unloaded, with no ammo.

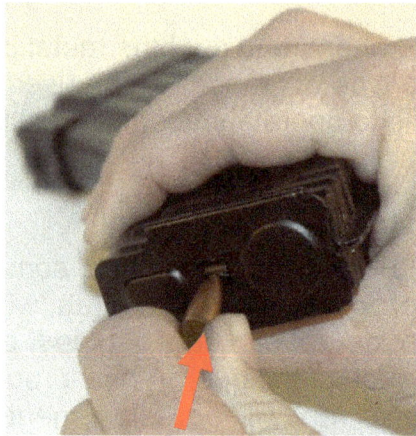

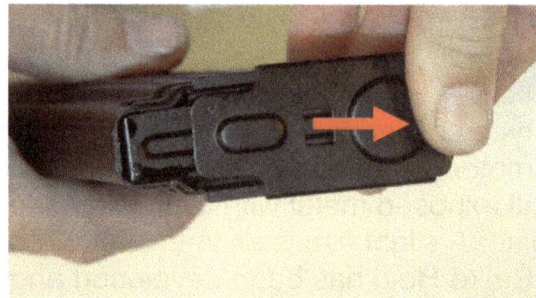

Figure 2-28a **Figure 2-28b**
Magazine floorplate removal

1- Use a bullet or pointed object to depress the retaining plate through the floor plate and start to slide the floor plate to the rear. The older, dirtier, and/or rusty the magazine is, the harder this step will be to do. Be careful not to slide the floor plate fully off until you are ready to apply pressure to the retainer plate, as it is under spring tension (Figures 2-28a and 2-28b).

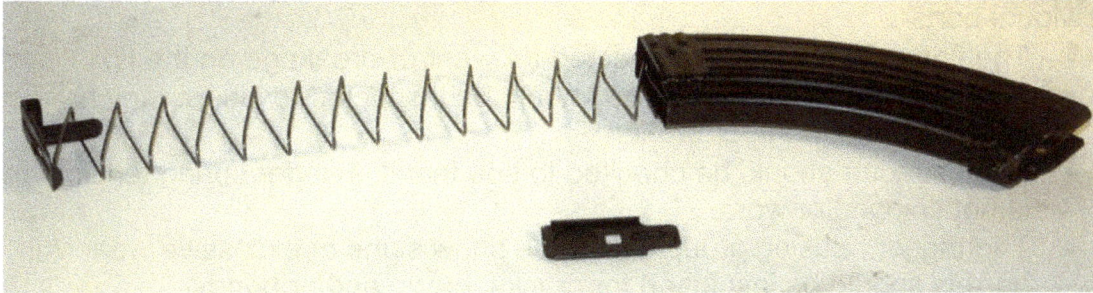

Figure 2-29a Magazine partial disassembled

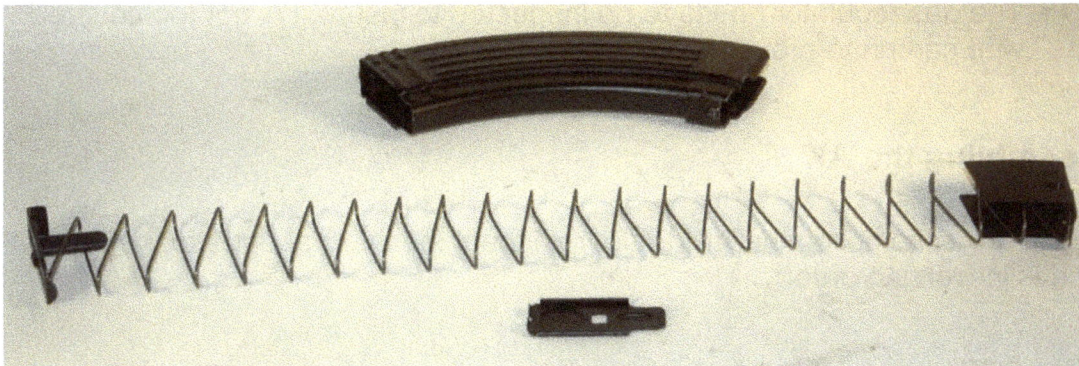

Figure 2-29b Magazine completely disassembled

2- Once you have the floor plate started, use your thumb to hold the retainer plate and remove the floor plate fully. Now you can release the spring tension in a controlled manner and remove the spring and follower from the magazine body. The follower and retaining plate can be removed from the spring if needed for thorough cleaning (Figures 2-29a and 2-29b).

It is very important to clean the inside of the magazine body and the outside of the follower. Keep the magazine as dry as possible but lightly coated with a protectant to prevent rusting.

To reassemble, just reverse the process.

Inspecting the AKM

To insure an AKM is serviceable and ready for action, it needs to be inspected periodically and between firings. This inspection can take place while the operator is cleaning the weapon. Disassemble as per the previous section and organize the parts in groups to be inspected.

Parts to inspect:
The overall condition of the weapon and components.

Individual parts-
- The firing pin should be inspected for wear or breakage on the tip.
- The mainspring and guide rod should be inspected to insure they have not been chipped, bent, or broken.
- The extractor should be checked to see that it is under spring tension and is not chipped or worn.
- The trigger housing group should no show signs of excessive wear. All barrels should be inspected for cracks, burrs, and or bends.
- The gas-piston cover should be inspected to see if it has any dents that would impede the movement of the gas piston during firing.
- The gas regulator needs to be inspected to insure it is not too covered with carbon to prevent adjustment.

Assembling the AK

As you are assembling the AKM rifle, reinspect the internal parts to insure that each is in working order.

Function Check Procedures

- Place the weapon on FIRE.
- Pull the charging handle to the rear and return it to its forward position.
- Place the weapon on SAFE.
- Pull the trigger; nothing should happen.
- Place the weapon on the semi-automatic selector position.
- Pull the trigger, and the hammer should release; hold the trigger back.
- Pull the charging handle to the rear and release; let up on the trigger and press it to release the hammer.
- Pull the charging handle to the rear and release, and place the weapon on the automatic-selector position.
- Pull the trigger (hold the trigger back), and the hammer should release.
- Pull the charging handle back, let up on the trigger, and you should not hear any hammer movement.
- Pull the cocking handle to the rear and return it to its forward position.
- Place the weapon on SAFE.

Section 3

Operation and Function

Loading the AK 30-round magazine

Ensure the magazines are clean, rust free, and without damage. Observe basic safety precautions of handling small arms ammunition at all times.

Figure 3-1 Loaded magazine

A. Ensure you have 7.62 x 39mm or 5.45 x 39mm ammunition; this ammunition is easily confused for with 7.62 x 51mm NATO (.308 Winchester) and 5.56 x 45mm NATO (.223 Remington). Inspect it for uniformity, cleanliness, and serviceability. Check all for undented primers and only use issued ammunition.

Figure 3-2a   **Figure 3-2b**   **Figure 3-2c**
Magazine loading procedure

A. Use your non-dominant hand to hold the magazine with the front of the magazine toward your fingertips. With your dominant hand, one at a time, place the cartridge over the top of the magazine follower between the feed lips and press the cartridge straight down until it snaps under the feed lips. Once the cartridge is under the lip of the magazine body, slide it fully to the rear so the next round will be allowed to be pushed down (Figures 3-2a, 3-2b and 3-2c).

B. The magazine can hold 30 cartridges, but due to overloading of the spring this should not be done; load 29 and then load the chamber so you have 28 in the magazine and one in the chamber. It is easiest to lay out the number of rounds for each magazine so you don't have to count the rounds as you load the magazine.

Drum Magazines

Developed primarily for the RPK, drums were developed to hold a very large amount of ammunition to reduce the number of magazine changes necessary during long bursts. Since the RPK in 7.62 x 39mm can accept both 7.62 x 39mm drums and AK magazines, the drum is capable of being used in the AK, though it was not the original intent. It is used primarily as a novelty with the AK because tactically they are unsound, as they weigh a great deal more then a standard 30-round magazine, and make a rattling sound when walking or moving.

Loading the Russian-style 75-round drum

Figure 3-3 Russian style drum magazine parts

1- Magazine lips   2- Spring lever

Figure 3-4 Spring lever use to load

1- Place the drum on a hard surface with the lever side up. While pushing down on the drum, index the lever fully counter-clockwise (Figure 3-4).

Figure 3-5 Russian style drum magazine parts

2- Insert the cartridge into the magazine opening and release the spring lever (Figure 3-5).

3- Repeat above procedure until the magazine is loaded—up to 75 rounds.

To unload, index the level fully counter-clockwise and remove the cartridge.

Loading the Chinese-style 75-round drum

Figure 3-6 Chinese style drum magazine

Figure 3-7a   **Figure 3-7b**
Opening the rear cover

1- Detach the two clips holding the cover on and pull the cover down until the drum is open (Figure 3-7a and 3-7b).

Figure 3-8 Spring tension button

2- Push the button in the middle of the drum to release the spring tension.

Figure 3-9 Follower positioning

3- Locate the follower and hold the button down while rotating the spider clockwise until the follower is in its starting position (Figure 3-9).

Figure 3-10 Placement of rounds

4- Place cartridges in the slots, starting with the slots next to the follower and continuing around in a spiraling pattern towards the lips of the drum (Figure 3-10).

Figure 3-11 Fully loaded drum

5- Put the cartridges everywhere where they will fit until the drum is full. Once you are done, shut the cover on the drum (Figure 3-11).

Figure 3-12 Winding up the drum

6- Before using the drum in your AK, you will want to wind it. Locate the knob on the back of the drum and turn it clockwise between 3-4 turns until it is tight (Figure 3-12). If it's not tight enough, the spring will not push the cartridges up fast enough to cycle properly. If it's too tight, it will be too difficult for your bolt to strip the rounds out of the drum. You will want to find the right amount of spring pressure for your combination of rifle and drum. You can mark the back of the drum with the correct numbers of turns to keep track of each drum's tension requirements.

Loading the AK Rifle

NOTE: Keep the weapon oriented in a safe direction.

Clear the weapon as described in the previous section.

Figure 3-13 Preparing to load the rifle

1- Place the safety, located on the right-hand side of the weapon, to the fully up (SAFE) position.

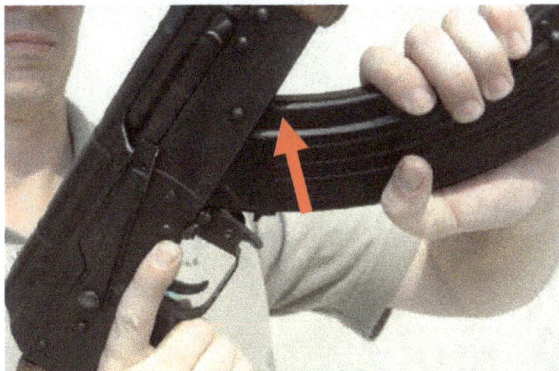

Figure 3-14a   **Figure 3-14b**
Inserting the magazine into the rifle

2- Insert the front of the magazine into the magazine well and rock the magazine to the rear to lock it in. Ensure it is locked into place by the magazine-release lever (Figure 3-14a and 3-14b).

Figure 3-15 Preparing to chamber a round

3- Place the weapon in a firing mode (either full or semi automatic mode) by sliding the selector/safety lever down. Down one is automatic and down two is semi automatic (Figure 3-15).

Figure 3-16a

Figure 3-16b

**Figure 3-16c
Charging the rifle**

4- Pull the charging handle fully back and release. As the bolt travels forward by the weapons spring tension, it will strip the top round from the magazine and force it into the chamber (Figures 3-16a, 3-16b and 3-16c).

Figure 3-17 Safety/Selector on SAFE

5- If you are preparing the rifle to fire, it is now ready; otherwise, return the selector/safety lever up into the safe position (Figure 3-17).

Figure 3-18 Press check

Press Check procedure-
To check if the chamber was loaded with a round, with the safety still engaged, pull the charging handle back to see the casing being pulled from the chamber (Figure 3-18). With the safety on, the charging handle will stop its rearward movement, and you can return the charging handle forward. In low-light, you may have to reach in and feel the cartridge casing to ensure the chamber is loaded.

Cycle of Function

Shooters can recognize and correct stoppages when they know how the AK/AKM Rifle functions. Each time a round is fired, the parts of the weapon function in a cycle or sequence. Many of the actions occur at the same time.

These actions are separated in this manual only for instructional purposes.

1. The semi-automatic cycle is started when the trigger is pulled. The sear is rotated forward and down, releasing the hammer. The hammer then rotates forward and strikes the firing pin. After firing, the bolt moves to the rear, rotating the hammer back toward the cocked position. The disconnector catches the hammer and holds it to the rear until the trigger is released. This action allows the sear to rotate back and engage the hammer and hold it in the cocked position for the next shot. The function of the disconnector is to make certain that another round cannot be fired until the trigger is released and pulled again.

2. The full-automatic cycle is started when the trigger is pulled. The sear is rotated forward and down, releasing the hammer. The hammer then rotates forward and strikes the firing pin. After firing, the bolt moves to the rear, rotating the hammer back toward the cocked position. The auto sear notch on the hammer catches on the auto sear and holds the hammer in the cocked position. As the weapon completes its cycle, during the last 1/2" of movement of the bolt carrier, the bolt carrier engages the auto sear and rotates it forward and down, releasing the hammer and starting the cycle again. This cycle continues until the trigger is released or the ammunition supply is exhausted.

3. The sequence of functioning is as follows:

    A. Firing. When the trigger is pulled, the hammer rotates and strikes the back of the firing pin where it protrudes from the back of the bolt. This drives the firing pin forward, and the tip of the firing pin protrudes through the firing pin hole in the bolt face and strikes the primer of the cartridge, and the primer fires the cartridge.

    B. Unlocking. After the cartridge is fired and the bullet passes the gas port, part of the expanding gases go into the gas block and from there, to the gas cylinder, forcing the piston to the rear. As the piston drives the bolt carrier to the rear, the cam surface engages the bolt, and it is rotated 45 degrees counter-clockwise, unlocking the bolt.

    C. Extracting. Extracting begins during the unlocking cycle. The rotation of the bolt loosens the cartridge case in the chamber. As the bolt and bolt carrier move to the rear, the extractor pulls the cartridge case from the chamber.

D. Ejecting. As the cartridge case is pulled from the chamber, the bolt passes by the ejector. The extractor grips the right side of the cartridge case and causes it to spin from the weapon as it reaches the ejection port.

E. Cocking. As the bolt carrier moves to the rear, it engages the hammer and rotates it back to the cocked position. At the same time, it compresses the operating spring.

F. Feeding. As the bolt starts its forward movement, it engages the rim of the next cartridge in the magazine. It then pushes that cartridge forward, and the cartridge is aligned with the chamber by the cartridge guide as the base of the cartridge clears the magazine feed lips.

G. Locking. As the cartridge is chambered, the bolt enters the barrel trunnion. As the cartridge is fully chambered, the extractor snaps over the rim of the case. As the bolt carrier continues forward, the cam surface engages the bolt and the bolt, is rotated 45 degrees clockwise, locking the bolt into the trunnion, and the weapon is ready to be fired again.

Firing the AKM

Orient toward the desired area/target, take a proper sight alignment and sight picture, rotate the selector/safety lever down to the desired fire position (one down for automatic and two down for semi-automatic), and press the trigger straight to the rear without interrupting your sight alignment and sight picture.

Once your target engagement is complete, rotate the selector to the rear SAFE position (up).

Proper Body Position to Fire

**Figure 3-19
Photo of standing position**

**Figure 3-20
Photo of kneeling position**

Figure 3-21 Photo of prone position

Figure 3-22 Supported barricade position

Carry and Ready Positions

Figure 3-23a   **Figure 3-23b**
Photos of carrying with three point and two point slings

Figure 3-24a   **Figure 3-24b**
Photos of low carry with thumb on safety/fire selector

Figure 3-25
Photo of high-ready position

Figure 3-26
Photo of low-ready position

Firing blanks from the AK rifle

To blank fire the AK type rifle, you must remove the flash suppressor/muzzle break and replace it with the appropriate blank firing adapter. AK-47 and AK-74 rifles have different adapters, and they are shown below.

The Blank Firing Adapter (BFA) replaces the flash suppressor to allow for the firing of blanks in training exercises. This item is available from www.VSSgear.com.

Figure 3-27
Photo of AK-47/AKM BFA

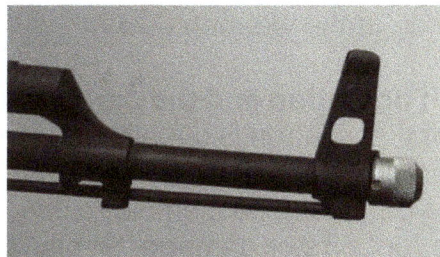

Figure 3-28
Photo of AK BFA on muzzle

To install, ensure the weapon is clear. Depress the spring-loaded detent and unscrew (reverse threaded - right direction) the slant muzzle break. Then screw (reverse threaded - left turn direction) the adapter on and depress the spring-loaded detent until tight and release the detent to fit one of the cutouts on the adapter.

Figure 3-29
Photo of AK-74 BFA

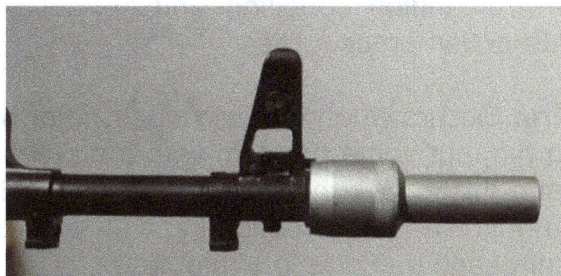

Figure 3-30
Photo of AK-74 BFA on muzzle

To install, ensure the weapon is clear. Depress the spring-loaded detent and unscrew (normal left direction) the slant muzzle break. Then screw (right turn direction) the adapter on and depress the spring-loaded detent until tight and release the detent to fit one of the cutouts on the adapter.

After blank fire, thoroughly clean all parts of the weapon which have had the powder fouling as this is very corrosive to untreated metal.

Section 4

Performance Problems

Malfunction and Immediate Action Procedures

A malfunction is a failure of the weapon to function properly. Defective ammunition or improper operation of the weapon by an operator is not considered a malfunction of the weapon.

Sluggish operation and the corrective action: Sluggish operation (gun fires very slowly) of the weapon is usually due to excessive friction caused by dirt or carbon, lack of proper lubrication, burred parts or excessive loss of gas. To correct this problem you must disassemble, clean, and lubricate the weapon while inspecting the parts for burrs or damage. Replace parts as necessary.

Stoppages: A stoppage is an interruption in the cycle of operation caused by a faulty gun or ammunition. In short, the gun stops firing. A stoppage must be cleared quickly by applying immediate action.

Immediate Action - This is the prompt action taken by the gunner to reduce a stoppage of the rifle without investigating the cause. If the gun stops firing, the shooter performs immediate action. Hang fire and cook off are two terms that describe ammunition condition and should be understood in conjunction with immediate-action procedures.

Hang Fire: Occurs when the cartridge primer has detonated after being struck by the firing pin, but some problem with the propellant powder causes it to burn too slowly, and this delays the firing of the projectile. Time (5 seconds) is allotted for this malfunction before investigating a stoppage further because of potential injury to personnel and damage to equipment.

Cook Off: Occurs when the heat of the weapon is high enough to cause the propellant powder inside the round to ignite even though the primer has not been struck. Immediate action is to unload the weapon immediately and allow it cool prior to reloading and firing.

Misfire Procedures

Immediate action: This action is performed when the operator has a failure to fire, which is when the trigger is pulled, the hammer moves forward, and the weapon does not fire. Recharge the rifle by pulling the charging handle to the rear, observe if a round is ejected, and release the charging handle to allow the action to close by its own spring tension. Attempt to refire, and if the weapon does not fire, take remedial action. If during your recharging of the action you observe a cartridge case or a round that is not ejected take remedial action.

Remedial Action: When immediate action fails to reduce the stoppage, remedial action must be taken. To do so tactically is to release the magazine; recharge the action 3-4 times, watching for the round to be extracted and ejected; reload the magazine into the weapon; charge the rifle; and attempt to refire. Administratively prior to investigating the cause of the stoppage, you must clear the weapon, and this step may involve some disassembly of the weapon and replacement of parts to correct the problem. Remedial actions for stoppages are as follows.

Stuck Cartridge: Some swelling of the cartridge occurs when it fires. If the swelling is excessive, the cartridge will be fixed tightly in the chamber. If the extractor spring has weakened and does not tightly grip the base of the cartridge, it may fail to extract a round when the bolt moves to the rear. Clear the weapon prior to this corrective action.

Insure the bolt is held to the rear and use the cleaning rod to punch down from the muzzle to dislodge the stuck casing. Prior to doing these actions, allow the weapon to cool if at all possible.

Ruptured Cartridge: Sometimes a cartridge is in a weakened condition after firing. In addition, it may swell as described above. In this case, a properly functioning extractor may sometimes tear the base of the cartridge off as the bolt moves to the rear, leaving the rest of the cartridge wedged inside the chamber. The ruptured cartridge extractor must be used in this instance to remove it.

Clear the weapon, disassemble the weapon up to, but do not remove the gas piston cover. Insert the shell extractor, which is attached to the cleaning rod, into the chamber to grip and remove the remains of the cartridge. Inspect the bore and reassemble the weapon.

Figure 4-1 Photo of cartridge extractor

Appendix A - Ammunition Comparison

9x18mm Makarov	9x19mm Luger	7.62x25mm Tokarev	.45 ACP

PISTOLS AND SUBMACHINE GUNS

Size Comparison of NATO vs. Non-Standard Ammunition

5.56x 45mm	5.45x 39mm	5.56x 45mm	7.62x 39mm	7.62x 51mm	7.62x 54R mm	12.7x 99mm	12.7x 108mm

ASSAULT RIFLES

SNIPER RIFLES & MACHINE GUNS

Appendix B - Non-Standard Ammunition Packaging & Markings

Packaging

Russian small arms cartridges are packed in sealed sheet-metal containers, with two containers per wooden crate. Older Russian production used rectangular containers of heavy gauge galvanized iron with soldered seams. Around 1959, the introduction of painted, rolled edge, rounded corner, tin plate 'sardine can' containers became the standard.

Metal and wooden crates have standardized markings that identify the contents as to caliber, functional type, cartridge case material, quantity and cartridge/powder lot data. Specialized cartridges are further identified by a color code consisting of one or two color stripes which correspond to bullet tip color. AP cartridges with tungsten carbide cores are identified by two concentric circles instead of color stripes. Russian cartridge designation, packaging and marking practices are generally followed by former Soviet-Bloc countries; each, however, has introduced some modifications in designation and marking. Russian ammunition packaging can be distinguished from Bulgarian packaging, which also carries Cyrillic markings, primarily by the different factory codes. The factory code on the container also appears in the headstamp of the cartridges in the container.

Steel Ammo Tins
(Sardine Cans)

Wood Ammo Crate (Case)
(Contains 2 Tins + Opener)

Cartridge quantities and weights of wooden crates

Country	Manufacturer	Caliber	Rounds /Crate	Crate Weight
Czech Rep.	Sellier and Bellot	14.5 x 114	210	53 kg.
India	OFB	14.5 x 114	60	15.5 kg.
Russia	Unknown	14.5 x 114	80	23 kg.
Bulgaria	Arsenal	12.7 x 108	200	29 kg.
Bulgaria	Arsenal	12.7 x 108	200	32 kg.
Pakistan	POF	12.7 x 108	280	42 kg.
Russia	Unknown	12.7 x 108	190	29 kg.
Russia	Novosibirsk	12.7 x 108	160	25 kg.
Bulgaria	Arsenal	7.62 x 54(R)	880	25 kg.
Czech Rep.	Sellier and Bellot	7.62 x 54(R)	800	24 kg.
Russia	Novosibirsk	7.62 x 54(R)	880	26 kg.
Russia	Novosibirsk	7.62 x 54(R)	600	21 kg.
Russia	Unknown	7.62 x 54(R)	880	26 kg.
Serbia	Prvi Partizan	7.62 x 54(R)	1,200	39 kg.
Czech Rep.	Sellier and Bellot	7.62 x 39	1,200	28 kg.
Pakistan	POF	7.62 x 39	1,750	39 kg.
Russia	Barnaul	7.62 x 39	1,320	30 kg.
Serbia	Prvi Partizan	7.62 x 39	1,260	29 kg.
Sudan	STC	7.62 x 39	1,500	28.1 kg.
Ukraine	Lugansk	7.62 x 39	1,320	30 kg.
Yugoslavia	Igman Zavod	7.62 x 39	1,260	28 kg.
Yugoslavia	Igman Zavod	7.62 x 39	1,120	27.5 kg.
Russia	Unknown	5.45 x 39	2,160	29 kg.
Ukraine	Lugansk	5.45 x 39	2,160	29 kg.

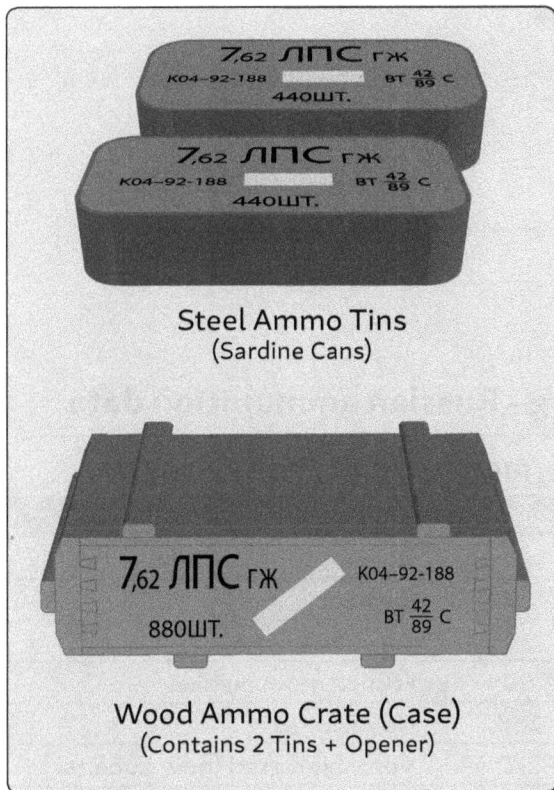

Non-Standard Ammunition tin and crate marking - diagrams

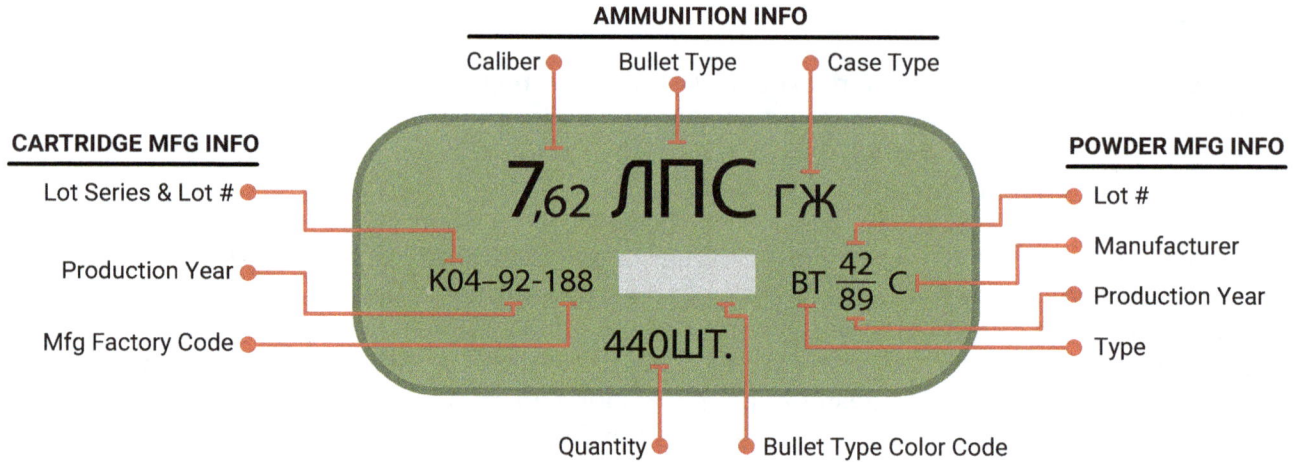

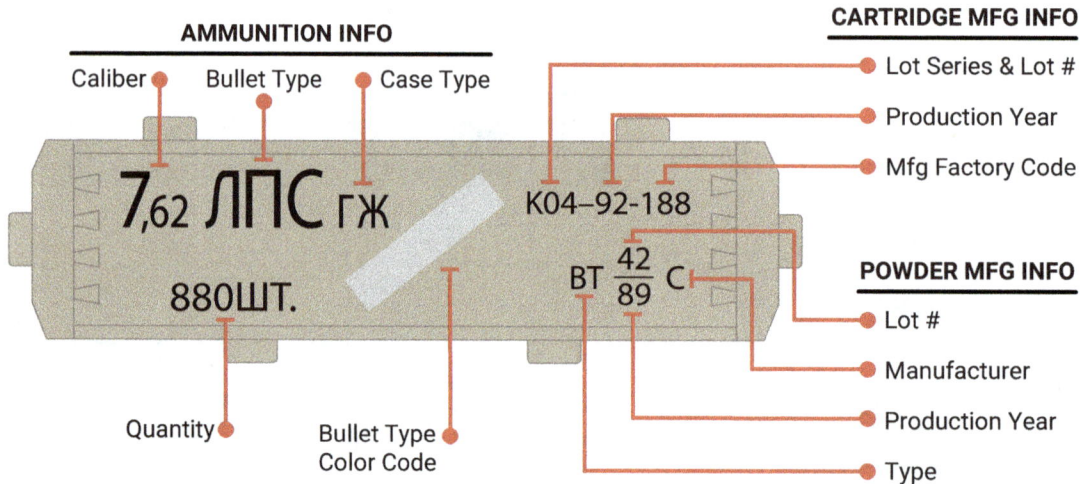

Non-Standard Ammunition tin and crate marking - Russian ammunition data

CASE TYPE MARKINGS

Mark	Meaning
ГЖ	Bimetallic case (gilding metal clad steel)
ГЛ	Brass case
ГС	Steel case

CARTRIDGE MFG FACTORY CODES

Code	Location
3	Ulyanovsk
17	Barnaul
38	Yuryuzan
60	Frunze (now Bishkek)
188	Novosibirsk
270	Voroshilovgrad (now Luhansk)
304	Lugansk
539	Tula
711	Klimovsk
T	Tula

Non-Standard Ammunition tin and crate marking - Russian ammunition data

BULLET TYPE MARKINGS

Mark	Meaning
Б Б-30 Б-32 БП	Armor-piercing
Б3	Armor-piercing incendiary
Б3Т Б3Т-44	Armor-piercing incendiary tracer
БС БС-40 БС-41	Armor-piercing with special core of tungsten carbide instead of carbon steel
БСТ	Armor-piercing with tungsten carbide core with added tracer
БТ	Armor-piercing tracer
Д	Heavy (long-range) with lead core instead of carbon steel
З ЗП	Incendiary
Л	Lightweight bullet
ЛПС	Light ball bullet with mild steel core
МДЗ	High explosive incendiary
П П-41	Spotting / ranging
ПЗ	Incendiary spotting / ranging
ПП	Enhanced penetration
ПС	Spotting / ranging with mild steel core
ПТ	Spotting / ranging tracer
СНБ	Armor-piercing sniper
Т Т-30 Т-45 Т-46	Tracer
57-У-322 57-У-323	Cartridge with higher powder charge
57-У-423	High-pressure cartridge
57-Х-322 57-Х-323 57-Х-340	Blank cartridge
57-НЕ-УЧ	Training cartridge
7Н1	Sniper bullet

BULLET TYPE COLOR CODES (Ammunition up to 14.5mm)

Color	Meaning
No color	Ball
White tip	Reference Ball
Silver tip	Light ball with steel core
Yellow tip	Heavy ball, or ball with torpedo base (on 7.62x54R)
Blue tip + white band	Short range ball 14.5x114 (only Hungarian and Czech)
Green tip + white band	Short range, tracer, (only Czech designation, only found on 7.62x39 with round nose)
Green tip	Tracer
Green tip & headstamp or entire cartridge green	Subsonic ammunition for silencer-weapons
Red tip	Spotting charge, incendiary
Red tip + white band	Short range tracer ball 14.5x114 (only Hungarian designation)
Entire bullet red	High explosive bullet (7.62x54R after 1945)
Entire bullet red	High explosive bullet (on 12.7 and 14.5mm)
Magenta tip + red band	Armor piercing incendiary tracer
Black tip + red band	Armor piercing incendiary
Black tip + red shell	Armor piercing incendiary with tungsten carbide core
Black tip + yellow band	Armor piercing incendiary Phosphorus 12.7
Black tip	Armor piercing

** The bullet tip color codes in the table above will be the same color codes on the tins or crates, but they will be color stripes on the packaging.

Example:

CARTRIDGE
Black Tip + Red Band

TIN or CRATE
Black Stripe + Red Stripe

Appendix C - Non-Standard Weapon Identification Markings

General Identification Markings

There are various identification markings found on non-standard weapons. Typically the markings will provide some or all of the following information:
- factory name or stamp (proof mark)
- caliber & serial number
- selector lever markings/symbols
- rear sight mark/symbol

Selector Lever Markings on Kalashnikov Rifles

Upper/ Safe Symbol	Mid/ Full-Auto Symbol	Lower/ Semi-Auto Symbol	Country
	Д	1	Albania
	L	D	Albania
	АВ	ЕД	Bulgaria
	L	D	China
	进	单	China
	30	1	Czechoslovakia
	آلي	وردي	Egypt
	D	E	Egypt
	D	E	East Germany
	∞	1	Hungary
آ	ص	م	Iraq
	련발	단발	North Korea
	C	P	Poland
	Z	O	Poland
S	A	R	Romania
S	FA	FF	Romania
	1	3	Romania
	ЛР	ОГОНЬ	Russia
	АВ	ОД	Russia
U	R	Ј	Yugo/Serbia

Rear Sight Marks on Kalashnikov Rifles

Symbol	Country
D	Albania
П	Bulgaria
D	China
N	East Germany
A	Hungary
Д	North Korea
S	Poland
P	Romania
П	Russia
O	Yugo/Serbia

NOTE: Data tables are not all inclusive, but they cover the more common weapon manufacturers.

Non-Standard Weapon Identification Markings

Factory Stamps and Countries of Manufacture

The table of symbols below are factory stamps (proof marks) for non-standard weapons. The symbols will identify the country of manufacture of the weapon. NOTE: *This is not an all inclusive list, but it covers the more common weapon manufacturers.*

(10) Bulgaria	(21) Bulgaria	(25) Bulgaria	China
(386) China	36 China	66 China	China
Egypt	East Germany	(3) East Germany	(K3) East Germany
East Germany	(06) East Germany	Iraq	Iraq
North Korea	North Korea	(11) Poland	Romania
Russia	Russia	Russia	Russia
Russia	Russia	Russia	Russia
Yugoslavia/Serbia	**M.70.AB2** Yugoslavia/Serbia	ZASTAVA-KRAGUJEVAC Yugoslavia/Serbia	

Appendix D - Non-standard weapons theory overview

There are three key concepts to understand when manipulating non-standard weapons. These simple and logical concepts are:

1. CYCLE OF OPERATIONS
2. OPERATING SYSTEMS
3. LOCKING SYSTEMS

> Firearm design trends are shared across region, manufacturer and class of weapon and are relatively obvious to recognize.
>
> Keep in mind that firearms are essentially simple machines that harness the energy created by the fired cartridge to operate the system.

CYCLE OF OPERATIONS (COO)

The cycle of operations is a crucial basis for understanding how the weapon operates and for function/malfunction diagnosis. Each specific malfunction will correspond to a specific step or sometimes two in the COO. A failure in the system at a certain point, will by default, cause a failure of omission of all subsequent steps. (example – a failure to properly extract will manifest as a failure to eject.)

The COO will vary based on the type of operating and locking systems. Once the operating and locking systems of the weapon are known, the COO is logical.

The examples below all start from a standard reference point: the weapon is loaded, charged, placed on fire and the trigger is pulled.

'Cycle of Operations' Examples:

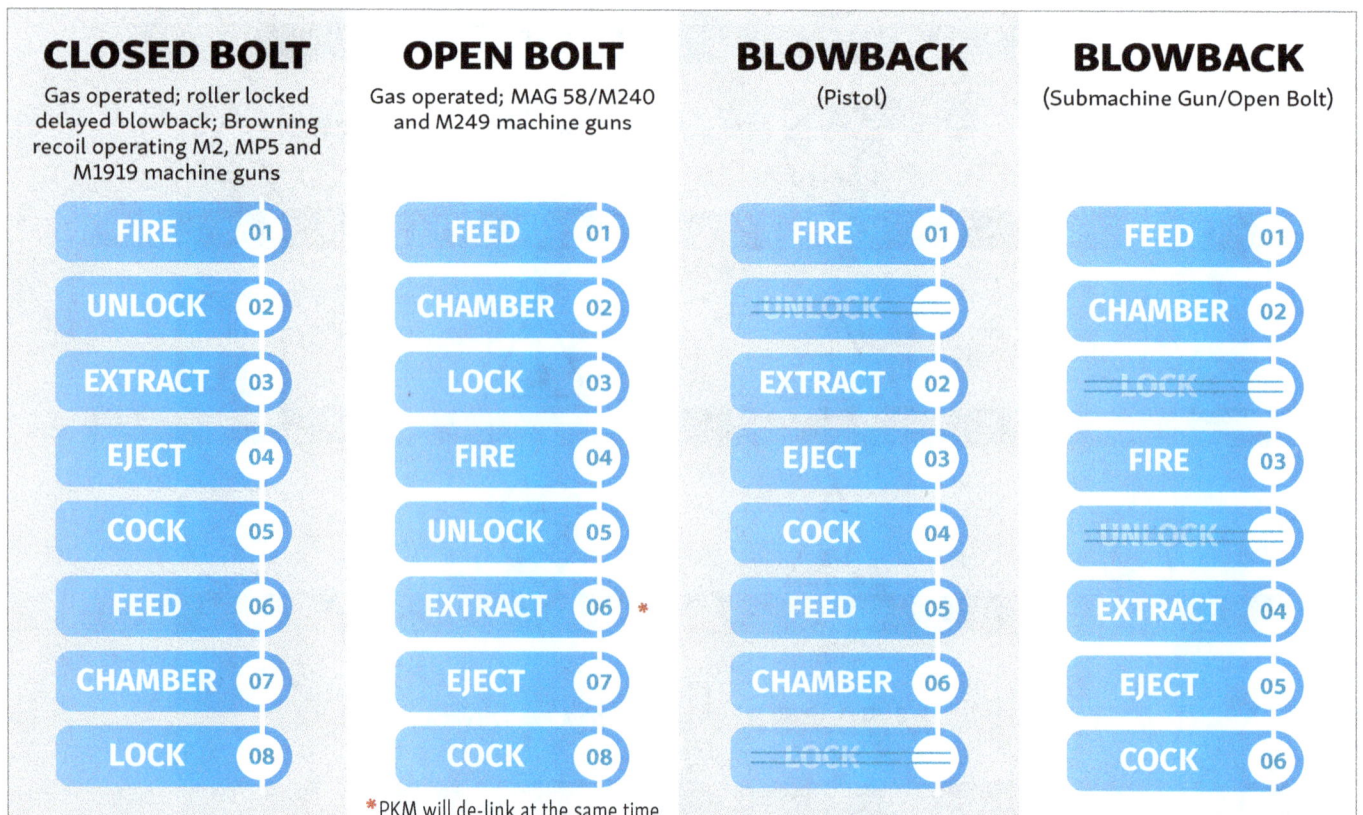

CLOSED BOLT	OPEN BOLT	BLOWBACK	BLOWBACK
Gas operated; roller locked delayed blowback; Browning recoil operating M2, MP5 and M1919 machine guns	Gas operated; MAG 58/M240 and M249 machine guns	(Pistol)	(Submachine Gun/Open Bolt)
FIRE 01	FEED 01	FIRE 01	FEED 01
UNLOCK 02	CHAMBER 02	~~UNLOCK~~	CHAMBER 02
EXTRACT 03	LOCK 03	EXTRACT 02	~~LOCK~~
EJECT 04	FIRE 04	EJECT 03	FIRE 03
COCK 05	UNLOCK 05	COCK 04	~~UNLOCK~~
FEED 06	EXTRACT 06 *	FEED 05	EXTRACT 04
CHAMBER 07	EJECT 07	CHAMBER 06	EJECT 05
LOCK 08	COCK 08	~~LOCK~~	COCK 06

*PKM will de-link at the same time

Non-standard weapons theory overview *(continued ...)*

⚙ OPERATING SYSTEMS

1. **Direct Impingement**- a type of gas operation that directs gas from a fired cartridge directly to the bolt carrier or slide assembly to cycle the action. (AR-15/M4 variants)

2. **Long-stroke piston system**- the piston is mechanically fixed to the bolt group and moves through the entire operating cycle. (AK variants)

3. **Short-stroke piston system (tappet system)**- the piston moves separately from the bolt group. It may directly push the bolt group parts as n the M1 carbine or operate through a connecting rod. (HK 416, AR180, POF, LWRC, FN FAL)

4. **Blowback**- the system of operation for self-loading firearms that obtains energy from the motion of the cartridge case as it is pushed to the rear by expanding gases created by the ignition of the propellant charge. (STEN, Makarov, M3 Grease Gun)

5. **Short recoil action**- the barrel and slide recoil only a short distance before they unlock and separate. The barrel stops quickly, and the slide continues rearward compressing the recoil spring and performing extraction, ejection and finally feeding a fresh round from the magazine in the counter recoil phase. During the last portion of its forward travel, the slide locks into the barrel and pushes the barrel back into battery. *(This is found in most handguns chambered for 9x19mm Parabellum or greater caliber. Smaller calibers, 9x18mm Makarov and below, generally use the blowback method of operation due to lower chamber pressure and associated simplicity of design.)

6. **Roller-locked, delayed-blowback**- when the bolt is closed, the rollers carried in the bolt are wedged into the receiver recesses. On firing, the rollers must be forced out of the recesses at great mechanical disadvantage, delaying the opening of the bolt, even with full power 7.62mm NATO (.308 Winchester) rifle cartridges used in the G3/HK 91 (G3, HK 91, HK 93, HK 53, MP5 variants)

7. **Inertia operated systems**- the bolt body is separated from the locked bolt body to remain stationary while the recoiling gun and locked bolt head moves rearward. This movement compresses the spring between the bolt head and bolt body, storing the energy required to cycle the action. Benelli shotguns.

Non-standard weapons theory overview *(continued ...)*

🔒 LOCKING SYSTEMS

1. **None** - all blowback pistols and some submachine guns – (STEN, UZI, M3 Grease Gun, Makarov, and CZ 82)

2. **Roller** - (HK variants, MG3, MG34, MG 42 and CZ 52)

3. **Rotating bolt** - (AK, Stoner, M60, and M249)

4. **Tilting bolt** - (SKS, FN FAL and MAG 58/M240)

5. **Tilting barrel** - (Tokarev TT33, Sig variants, M1911 variants and Glock variants)

6. **Rotating barrel** - (MAB P15, Colt All American 2000, and Beretta 8000)

7. **Locking flaps** - (RPD, DP/DPM and DShK)

8. **Falling locking block** - (P38, M9, and VZ58)

Function check
Checking the mechanical function of a weapon by replicating, without ammunition, the firing modes from the lowest rate of fire (SAFE if applicable) to the highest in a progressive sequence (not by selector location). The parts checked are the safety/safeties, sear and disconnector.

M4A1
1. Ensure the rifle is clear
2. Charge and place the weapon on SAFE
3. Attempt to fire (weapons should not FIRE, safety is functioning)
4. Place the weapon on SEMI, pull the trigger and hold it to the rear (hammer should fall, trigger/sear functioning)
5. Maintain the trigger to the rear and cycle the bolt
6. Release the trigger and listen for a metallic click (disconnector functioning)
7. Pull the trigger again and the hammer should fall
8. Charge the weapon and place on AUTO
9. Pull the trigger and hold it to the rear then cycle the bolt more than once
10. Release the trigger and pull it again, nothing should happen (auto sear is functioning)
11. Charge the weapon then pull the trigger again and the hammer should fall
12. Function check complete

Significant visual indicators
- Any checked, knurled or serrated surface
- Any movable lever or switch
- Pins with gripping surfaces
- Index marks (two lines that need to be aligned to disassembled (CZ 75)
- Recoil spring with ends of different diameters

www.ingramcontent.com/pod-product-compliance
Lightning Source LLC
Chambersburg PA
CBHW080519110426
42742CB00017B/3174